GEOGRAPHY FOR COMMON ENTRANCE

Second Edition

John Widdowson

Hodder Murray

A MEMBER OF THE HODDER HEADLINE GROUP

The author would like to thank Paul Baker, Fiona Langridge, Andrew Lee and Simon Lewis for their contribution to this book.

Although every effort has been made to ensure that website addresses are correct at time of going to press, Hodder Murray cannot be held responsible for the content of any website mentioned in this book. It is sometimes possible to find a relocated web page by typing in the address of the home page for a website in the URL window of your browser.

Hodder Headline's policy is to use papers that are natural, renewable and recyclable products and made from wood grown in sustainable forests. The logging and manufacturing processes are expected to conform to the environmental regulations of the country of origin.

Orders: please contact Bookpoint Ltd, 130 Milton Park, Abingdon, Oxon OX14 4SB. Telephone: (44) 01235 827720. Fax: (44) 01235 400454. Lines are open 9.00–5.00, Monday to Saturday, with a 24-hour message answering service. Visit our website at www.hoddereducation.co.uk

© John Widdowson 2007
First published in 2003 by
Hodder Murray, an imprint of Hodder Education and
a member of the Hodder Headline Group, An Hachette Livre UK Company
338 Euston Road
London NW1 3BH

Reprinted 2003 (twice), 2004, 2006
This second edition published 2007

Impression number	5 4 3 2 1
Year	2010 2009 2008 2007

Cover: *main photo* © Douglas Peebles/Robert Harding Picture Library; *from top* © John Widdowson; © dpa/Corbis; © Digital Vision/Getty Images; © John Widdowson; © Ecoscene/ Frank Blackburn

Typeset in RotisSerif 11.5/13pt
Layouts by Amanda Easter
Artwork by Oxford Designers & Illustrators Ltd
Printed and bound in Italy
A catalogue entry for this book is available from the British Library.

ISBN 978 0 340 93979 6
Teacher's Resource Book 978 0 340 93978 9

Contents

This symbol shows the best opportunities for developing your ICT skills alongside your geography work.

Key words – new geographical words are printed in blue letters. These are words that you really need to know. The glossary at the back of the book tells you their meanings.

Acknowledgements

Photos

p.1 © Mike Page; p.3 Leo Mason/Action Plus; p.4 *tr* Gary Smith/Collections, *tl* GeoScience, *bl* Worldwide Picture Library/Alamy; p.7 *b* London Aerial Photo Library; p.8 Mark Edwards/Still Pictures; p.10 © Terry Bottomley/Alamy; p.16 John Giles/PA Photos; p.17 geogphotos/Alamy; p.20 *t* Geoscience, *c* Sealand Aerial Photography, *b* Rex Features; p.22 © Vincent Laforet/epa/Corbis; p.23 © Robert Galbraith/Reuters/Corbis; p.25 © Vincent Laforet/Pool/Reuters/Corbis; p.26 © Digitalglobe via CNP/CNP/Corbis; p.27 *l* © Smiley N. Pool/Dallas Morning News/ Corbis, *r* AP/Eric Gay/Empics; p.29 Steve Hall/Rex Features; p.30 David Ducros/Science Photo Library; p.31 *tr* Popperfoto, *l* Quentin Bates/Ecoscene, *b* George Montgomery/Photofusion; p.32 Cape Grim B.A.P.S./Simon Fraser/Science Photo Library; p.41 *t* Robert Hallmann/Collections, *b* C.Stadtler/Photofusion; p.42 *b* Vincent Lowe, *t* Vincent Lowe; p.44 NERC Satellite Station, University of Dundee; p.45 Kathy Wright/Alamy; p.46 Arco Images/Alamy; p.48 © Laurent Dominique/epa/Corbis; p.50 *r* PurestockX; p.53 © Lester Lefkowitz/Corbis; p.54 *t* Yorkshire Television, *b* © BBC; p.55 *t* © FremantleMedia, *b* © FremantleMedia; p.57 *t* © Jason Hawkes Aerial Photography, *c* © Jason Hawkes Aerial Photography, *b* © Jason Hawkes Aerial Photography; p.59 *t* Aerofilms, *c* Courtesty of East Riding of Yorkshire Council, *b* Courtesty of East Riding of Yorkshire Council; p.60 *t* © John Phillips/Alamy, *b* © Skyscan; p.63 *cb* Ian M Butterfield/Alamy; p.65 *tr* © gary718 – Fotolia, *br* Santiago Castrillon/Photofusion, *tl* Alex Segre/Alamy, *bl* Liz Stares/Collections; p.66 *t* Bridgeman Art Library, *b* Alain Le Garsmeur/Collections; p.69 *t* G.Horner/Art Directors & Trip Photo Library; p.70 Adrian Dennis/AFP/Getty Images; p.72 Skyscan/© Bluesky-World; p.73 Scott Barbour/Getty Images; p.74 ©Molly Cooper/Photofusion; p.75 *l* Adrian Dennis/AFP/Getty Images, *r* Stuart Clarke/Rex Features; p.76 Alan Copson City Pictures/ Alamy; p.77 M-SAT LTD/Science Photo Library; p.78 Andrew Butterton/Alamy; p.79 VIEW Pictures Ltd/Alamy; p.81 *l* The Photo Library Wales/Alamy, *r* Christoph Rosenberger/Alamy; p.82 Neal Simpson/Empics; p.83 Mike Egerton/Empics; p.84 *cr* Quentin Bates/Ecoscene; p.84 *t* Bob Gibbons/Holt/FLPA, *cl* Public Record Office Image Library, *b* Gordon Roberts/Holt/FLPA; p.85 *t* Roger Bamber/Alamy, *c* James Holmes/Reed Nurse/Science Photo Library, *b* ImageState/Alamy; p.86 *bl* © Frithjof Hirdes/zefa/ Corbis, *br* Martin Jenkinson/Alamy, *tl* Mary Evans Picture Library, *tr* Chris Knapton/Ecoscene; p.87 Topfoto; p.88 *tc* Zak Waters/Alamy, *bl* Jochen Tack/Alamy, *tr* Andrew Parker/Alamy, *br* Philip Corbluth/Alamy, *bc* Photofusion Picture Library/Alamy, *tl* Matthew Ashton/Empics; p.90 *t* London Aerial Photo Library, *c* © constructionphotography.com, *b* London Aerial Photo Library; p.93 Ferruccio/Alamy; p.94 Doug Martin/Science Photo Library; p.96 Courtesy of Toyota Motor Manufacturing (UK) Ltd; p.98 WoodyStock/Alamy; p.100 Fethi Belaid/AFP/Getty Images; p.102 *l* ImageState/Alamy, *r* AP/Brennan Linsley/Empics, *c* ImageState/ Alamy; p.103 *t* The FAIRTRADE Mark is a Certification Mark and a registered trademark of Fairtrade Labelling Organisations International (FLO) of which the Fairtrade Foundation is a member, *l* Simon Rawles/Alamy, *c* © Hug, reproduced with kind permission, *r* © Hug, reproduced with kind permission; p.105 © Bryand & Cherry Alexander Photography; p.108 Worldsat Productions/NRSC/Science Photo Library; p.109 *ct* © Skyscan, *b* Andrew Davies/Still Pictures; p.109 *t* Peak District National Park Authority/Mike Williams/Peak Pictures, *cb* Peak District National Park Authority/Mike Williams/Peak Pictures; p.110 *tl* Warwick Sloss/Nature Pl.com, *tr* Collections/John & Eliza forder; p.111 Dietmar Nill/Naturepl.com; p.112 Edward Parker/Still Pictures; p.113 Mark Edwards/Still Pictures; p.116 John Duckett/Alamy; p.117 London Aerial Photo Library; p.118 *t* David Bowie/Collections, *b* Michael Howell/Alamy; p.120 *t* UNICEF, *c* Jeff Stanfield, *r* Jeff Stanfield; p.121 *t* Jeff Stanfield, *b* UNICEF; p.123 Chinch Gryniewic/Ecoscene; p.124 *l* © iStockphoto.com/ Carl Hancock, *r* © Pilar Olivares/Reuters/Corbis; p.127 © iStockphoto.com/gioadventures, *tl* © iStockphoto.com/Tomasz Resiak, *bl* Hemis/Alamy, *br* PurestockX,; p.129 *l* © Reuters/Corbis, *r* © Pawel Kopczynski/Reuters/Corbis; p.131 © SUPRI/Reuters/ Corbis; p.132 *t* Kevin Schafer/Still Pictures, *b* © MAST IRHAM/ epa/Corbis; p.133 © Patrick Roberts/Sygma/Corbis; p.134 Geospace/Science Photo Library; p.135 *l* Douglas Peebles/Robert Harding Picture Library, *r* Rex Features; p.136 Andrew Lambert Photography; p.137 *t* © Bettman/Corbis, *b* Gerard & Margi Moss/ Still Pictures; p.140 Digital Globe, Eurimage/Science Photo Library; p.141 *l* Digital Globe, Eurimage/Science Photo Library, *r* © Yusuf Ahmad/Reuters/Corbis; p.144 AP/Dita Alangkara/Empics; p.145 Mary Evans Picture Library; p.146 Sipa Press/Rex Features; p.147 Rex Features–Butler/Bauer A/C; p.149 Gavin Hellier/Robert Harding Picture Library; p.157 © Patrick Robert/Sygma/Corbis.

t = top, *b* = bottom, *l* = left, *r* = right, *c* = centre

Text

p.88 Pocket World in Figures 2007 (Economist) © Profile Books Ltd; p. 97 © The Automobile Association Developments Limited 2007 LIC003/07 A03397 © Crown copyright. All rights reserved. Licence number 100021153; p.100 Adapted from 'Story of the Blues', © Fran Abrams and James Astill; All Ordnance Survey material reproduced by permission of Ordnance Survey on behalf of HMSO. © Crown Copyright 2007. All rights reserved. Ordnance Survey Licence number 100036470.

Every effort has been made to contact copyright holders, but if any have been inadvertently overlooked, the publishers will be pleased to make the necessary arrangements at the earliest opportunity.

Geomorphological Processes

Coasts, rivers and glaciers

▲ The cliffs at Happisburgh (say Hays-borough) on the Norfolk coast

These houses don't look very safe on these cliffs, but this coastline didn't always look this way.

- Would you like to live here? Why?
- Where do you think the coastline was a few years ago?
- Where will it be a few years from now?
- What is causing the landscape to change?

1.1   Is your school breaking up?

Nothing stays the same for ever. Everything – even the landscape – changes. Most of these changes are so slow that you might not notice them taking place, but over thousands of years even the most solid rock can change. All the forces of nature – sun, water, ice and air – bring about changes to the landscape, breaking up the surface and wearing it away.

▲ **A** Paint peels from walls, doors and window frames. Changes of temperature – especially if the weather is very hot or very cold – cause paint to expand and to shrink. This makes it crack and peel from the surface beneath.

All the processes that change the natural landscape also work on buildings. They are probably happening in your school. Sun, rain, frost, wind and even plants can attack buildings, causing them to break up or crumble. This process is called weathering.

▲ **C** Plants such as mosses and lichens grow on roofs and walls. They send their roots into the tiles or bricks, which makes them slowly crumble. As the surface breaks up, it makes way for larger plants to grow.

▲ **B** Cement crumbles. Rain, which behaves like a very weak acid, slowly eats away at the cement between the bricks.

Another process that changes the landscape is erosion. In the natural landscape this is mainly due to rivers, the sea, ice or wind wearing away rock.

People are also an important cause of erosion. The more people that move over a surface the quicker it is likely to be eroded. Look at this football pitch at the end of the football season (photo D).

▲ **D** Erosion on a football pitch

Activities

I Look at photos A, B and C. Each one shows a different type of weathering. Match each photo with a type of weathering:

- **Physical weathering** – caused by changes in temperature
- **Chemical weathering** – caused by the action of water
- **Biological weathering** – caused by the action of plants or animals.

2 Investigate your own school, or your local area. How many examples of weathering can you find?
  a) Draw sketches to show any examples that you find.
  b) Suggest the cause of weathering in each case.

3 Look at photo D.
  a) Describe the pattern of erosion on the football pitch, or, if you prefer, you can draw it.
  b) Explain the pattern that you can see.

4 Think about another sport that you play on grass. It could be cricket, hockey, rugby, tennis or another sport.
  a) Draw a plan of the pitch.
  b) Shade all the areas that are likely to be eroded on your plan.

1.2 **Shaping the landscape**

Weathering and erosion work together to shape the natural landscape. Weathering breaks up the Earth's surface. Erosion also wears away the surface and transports the loose rock elsewhere. Water, ice and wind all erode the landscape. Over thousands of years they slowly change its shape. Each type of erosion produces its own particular landforms.

▲ **A** Rivers erode the landscape to form V-shaped valleys

▲ **B** The sea meets the land at the coast. Waves slowly shape the coastline, forming bays and headlands.

▲ **C** Glaciers are slow-moving rivers of ice. When glaciers melt, they leave deep U-shaped valleys.

Activities

1 Study photos A–C showing three types of erosion – river, coastal and glacial.
   a) Name the landforms produced by each type of erosion.
   b) Which type of erosion do you think is most powerful? Explain your choice.
2 Look at the drawings in D. Match each drawing with one of the descriptions below. Write them in your book with the correct heading.
   • Rocks and stones bump into each other and get worn down to sand or shingle.
   • Waves hammer into cracks in the rock, forcing it to split apart.
   • Some rocks dissolve slowly in water.
   • Waves throw rocks and stones at the cliff, wearing it away like sandpaper.

River and coastal erosion both work in similar ways. The drawings in D show waves eroding land at the coast. The same processes happen in rivers. You can find out more about how glaciers erode on pages 10–11.

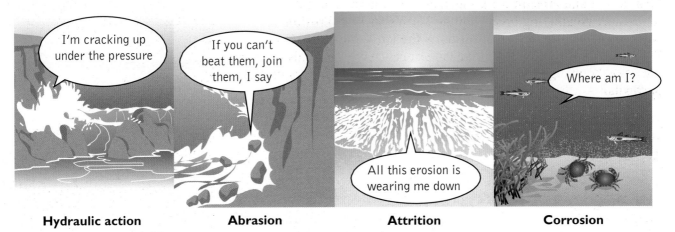

Hydraulic action   **Abrasion**   **Attrition**   **Corrosion**

▲ **D** Four ways in which waves erode the land

3 Look at photos E and F. They show two cliffs – one made of hard rock, the other of soft rock.
   a) How can you tell which is which?
   b) Draw sketches of the two photos. Choose the correct labels from the box below to add to the sketches. Give each sketch a suitable title.

cliff made of hard rock	cliff made of soft rock
waves slowly erode cliff	waves quickly erode cliff

Homework

4 Find out how difficult it is to erode different types of material. Find small samples of different materials at home. Here are some materials you could try: chalk, wood, glass, soap, brick, metal.

Rub each one with sandpaper. How easily do they erode?

List the materials in order of how difficult they are to erode, with the hardest at the top.

▶ **E** Chalk cliffs at Beachy Head, Sussex

▲ **F** Clay cliffs on East Yorkshire coast

1.3   Changing coastline

The sea is constantly changing the shape of the land. When Julius Caesar, commander of the Roman army, landed in Britain over 2,000 years ago, the coastline on which he landed was not the same as it is today. Places which were on the coast then are no longer there. Some have disappeared altogether, washed away as the sea has eroded the land. Others are now found far inland, where the sea has built up new land.

FUNNY...I'M SURE I LEFT MY SHIP SOMEWHERE ROUND HERE!

In stormy weather, large waves crash against the coast and erode it. Sea currents transport the eroded rocks and sand along the coast and deposit it in calmer water. These processes – erosion, transportation and deposition – are happening all around the coast.

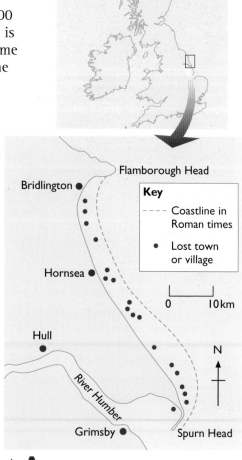

▲ **A** East Yorkshire coast

Activities

1 Look at map A. Then look at the photos on page 7.
   a) On a copy of the map, label a place where
      i) erosion, and ii) deposition, happens.
   b) Draw an arrow on the map to show the direction in which the sea transports material.
   c) Today, Bridlington is a seaside resort (photo D on page 59). It wasn't 2,000 years ago. What do you think has happened?

2 Look at photos B, C and D. Compare them with drawing E.
   a) Identify the landforms shown in the photos.
   b) Draw a simple sketch of each photo. Label the landforms.
   c) Complete these sentences to explain how the landform in each photo was made.

Choose words from the box below. You can use some words twice.

cave   stack   cracks   arch

Waves crash against a headland and attack _____ in the rock. They grow wider to form a _____.
When a _____ is eroded all the way through the headland it turns into an _____.
Eventually, further erosion causes the roof of the _____ to collapse. It leaves a _____ standing in the sea.

3 Look at photo F.
   Write a short paragraph to explain how Spurn Head has been made. Use the words – *erode, transport* and *deposit* – in your explanation.

▲ **B**

▲ **C**

▲ **D**

The coast near Flamborough Head is being eroded

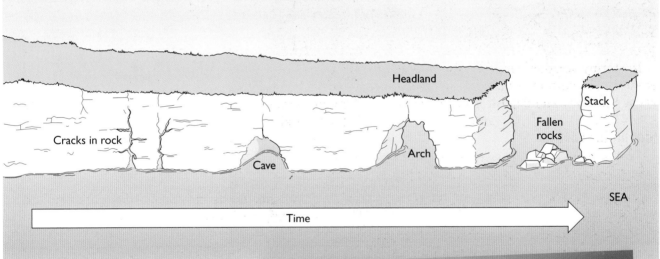

▲ **E** Stages in the erosion of a headland

The sea deposits the material it has eroded around the coast to form beaches. The material can be any size from the finest sand to large stones. Waves transport it along the coast by the process of longshore drift.

Sometimes longshore drift continues across a bay or river mouth to form a spit. Spurn Head is a spit deposited across the mouth of the River Humber (photo F).

▲ **F** Spurn Head, a spit formed by deposition

1.4   Rivers shape the land

Rivers change the shape of the land as they flow from source to mouth.

In the hills a fast-flowing river erodes down into its channel to make a valley. Weathering attacks the steep valley sides and widens them to form a V-shaped valley. In some places, where the river tumbles over harder rock, it forms waterfalls (C).

The river transports the material it has eroded. Fine material, like sand or mud, is carried in the water, making it look dirty. Heavy material, like rocks and pebbles, is rolled along the river bed. Some material is deposited along the way. As the river twists and turns it forms meanders (D).

▼ **A** A river valley from source to mouth

The river source

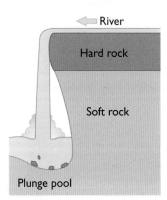

▲ **B** High Force, a waterfall on the River Tees in County Durham

← River

Hard rock

Soft rock

Plunge pool

Erosion undercuts the harder rock

Soft rock erodes more quickly

Hard rock collapses

The waterfall moves back

Rock is carried away by the river

Erosion continues and the waterfall slowly moves upstream

A gorge is left behind

▲ **C** Development of a waterfall

▶ **D** Cross-section of a meander

Water flows slowly around the inside of the bend

Water flows quickly around the outside of the bend

A gentle slope forms

Erosion on the outer bank

Deposition on the inner bank

The channel is shallow

The channel is deep

A river cliff forms

As it nears the river mouth, the valley widens. Flat land on either side of the river is called the flood plain. This is the area that the river floods when it overflows. It deposits fine mud called alluvium. Flood plains often have rich fertile soil that is good for farming.

Activities

1 Look at drawing A.

Write three sentences to describe the changes that happen between the source and mouth. You can start like this.

Near the source the river is narrow and fast-flowing, but near the mouth ...

Near the source the river erodes its channel ...

Near the source the valley is ...

2 Look at photo B.

a) Draw a sketch of the waterfall. Label these features:

> waterfall   plunge pool   layer of hard rock
> layer of soft rock

The information on diagram C will help you.

b) Mark the position on your sketch where you think the waterfall might be in future. Explain your choice.

3 Look at photo D.

a) Complete a large copy of this cross-section showing a meander.

Label these features on the cross-section:

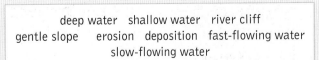

> deep water   shallow water   river cliff
> gentle slope   erosion   deposition   fast-flowing water
> slow-flowing water

b) How do you think the position of the meander will change with time?

1.5 The power of ice

It may be hard to believe, looking around you now, that most of Britain was once covered in ice (map A). During the Ice Age temperatures were much lower than they are today. Snow collected in the mountains in Britain and turned into glaciers – slow-moving rivers of ice (photo C on page 4). Ice sheets advanced across the British Isles from Scandinavia. Only southern England was not covered by ice, and even here the ground was frozen!

You can still see evidence of the Ice Age in the landscape today. Deep, U-shaped valleys were carved by the glaciers. Later, when the ice melted, lakes were left behind in the valleys. The Lake District in north-west England (photo B) is an example of a glacial landscape.

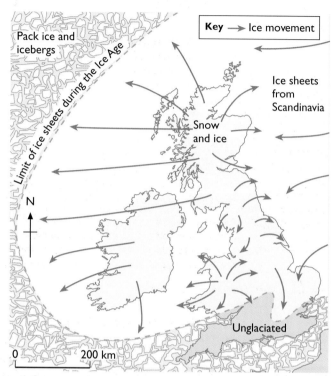

▲ **A** The British Isles during the Ice Age

▲ **B** Buttermere in the Lake District

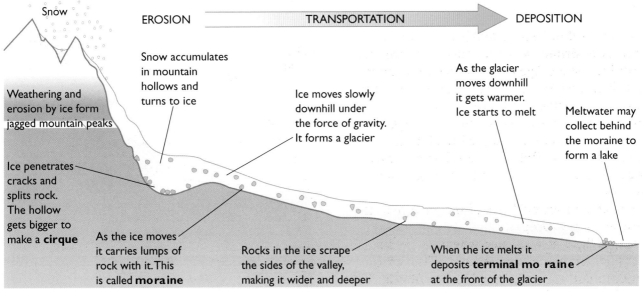

EROSION → TRANSPORTATION → DEPOSITION

Snow

Snow accumulates in mountain hollows and turns to ice

Weathering and erosion by ice form jagged mountain peaks

Ice moves slowly downhill under the force of gravity. It forms a glacier

As the glacier moves downhill it gets warmer. Ice starts to melt

Meltwater may collect behind the moraine to form a lake

Ice penetrates cracks and splits rock. The hollow gets bigger to make a **cirque**

As the ice moves it carries lumps of rock with it. This is called **moraine**

Rocks in the ice scrape the sides of the valley, making it wider and deeper

When the ice melts it deposits **terminal moraine** at the front of the glacier

▲ **C** Cross-section of a glacier

There are no glaciers in Britain today because our climate is too warm. However, ice is still changing the landscape in other parts of the world. Most of Antarctica and Greenland are covered by giant ice sheets. All the world's highest mountain ranges – like the Himalayas and the Andes – still have glaciers. There is evidence that, as the world gets warmer, glaciers are melting faster than they are being fed, causing glacial retreat.

Activities

I Look at map A.
  a) Name three cities that would have been covered by ice during the Ice Age.
  b) Name three cities that would not have been covered by ice.

  You can use an atlas to help you.

2 Look at photo B. The sketch below shows what the same landscape might have looked like during the Ice Age.

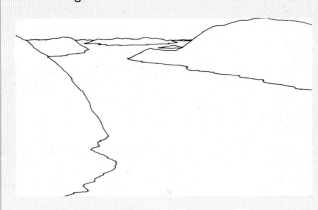

  a) Make a large copy of the sketch. Label the glacier.
  b) Now, draw a similar sketch of photo B. On your sketch, label the following features: a U-shaped valley, a mountain peak, a lake.

3 Study cross-section C. Explain how each of the features that you labelled in your sketch was formed:
  a) a U-shaped valley
  b) a mountain peak
  c) a lake.

1.6

What can you see beside the sea?

In this case study you will use a map and photos to identify coastal features, and explain how they were formed.

Holidays are a good time to do geography. Many people go to the seaside for their holiday, either in this country or abroad. If you go to the coast, you may be able to see some of the coastal landforms that you have met in this unit, and you could ask a few geographical questions – what is it, why is it there, and how is it changing?

Swanage is a popular holiday resort in Dorset, in the south of England. The photos on this page were taken on the coast in and around Swanage.

▲ A

▲ B

▲ C

▲ D

Activities

1   Look at photos A and B. What landforms can you identify?

2   Look at map E on the opposite page. It shows the coast near Swanage. Follow the south-west coast path from The Foreland (in grid square 0582) to Durlston Head (in grid square 0377).

Match each photo with one of these grid squares on the map: 0377, 0378, 0582, 0379. Give a name for the place in each photo.

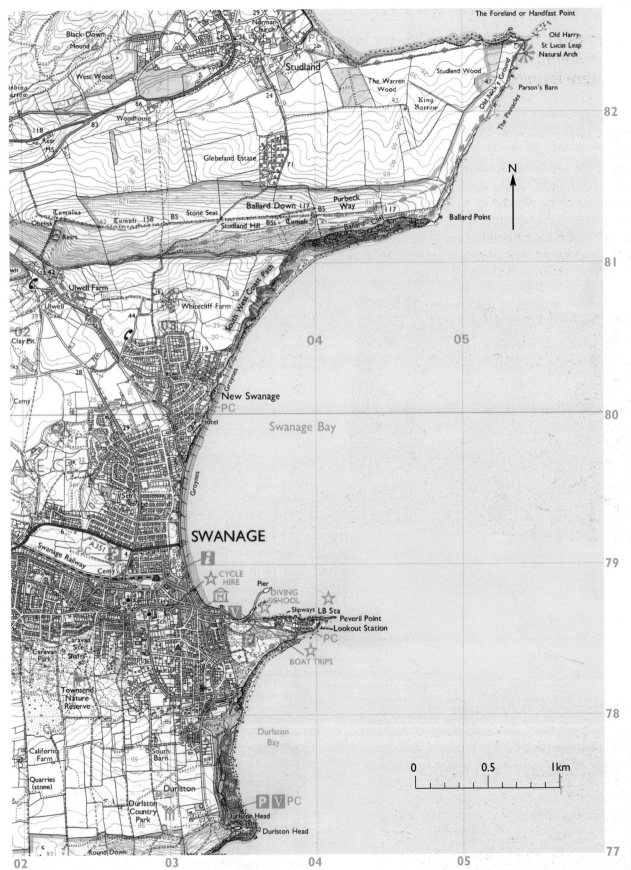

▲ **E** Swanage. Reproduced from the 2006 1:25,000 Ordnance Survey map of Swanage by permission of the Controller of HMSO © Crown Copyright.

Why is it there?

The geology, or rocks, around Swanage can help to explain the landforms that are found in the area. Like most of southern and eastern England, it is made of sedimentary rocks that were formed millions of years ago by material (or sediment) deposited on the sea bed. Each layer of rock represents a different period of geological history. Chalk, limestone, sandstone and clay are all types of sedimentary rock. Since they were laid down, the rocks have been pushed up and folded by powerful forces deep within the Earth.

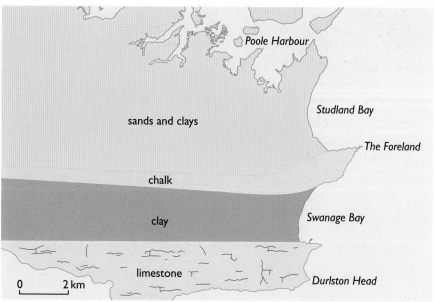

▲ **F** A geological map of the Swanage area

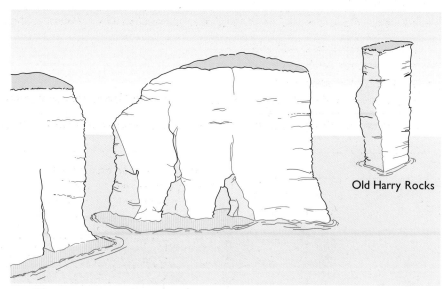

▲ **G** The Foreland, near Swanage

Activities

1 Look at map F. It is a geological map of the Swanage area.
   a) What type of rock is found around:
      i)   The Foreland
      ii) Swanage Bay
      iii) Durlston Head
      iv) Studland Bay?
   b) Which of these rocks do you think are hard, and which soft? Give your reasons.

2 Look at drawing G, which shows the Foreland as it is today.
   a) Draw a sketch to show what it may have looked like thousands of years ago. Explain any changes that have taken place.
   b) Draw another sketch to show what it may look like thousands of years from now. Explain why this may happen.

Activities

3 Plan a coastal walk, following the coast path, from the Foreland to Durlston Head. Use map E on page 13 to help you. Break the walk up into sections. For each section:

a) give six-figure grid references

b) measure the distance, using the scale

c) say in which direction you are walking

d) mention any interesting features that you pass.

Lay out your plan in a table, like this:

From	Grid ref	To	Grid ref	Distance	Direction	Interesting features
The Foreland	054 827	Ballard Point	048 813	1.5 km	SW	Old Harry

Assignment

Produce an information leaflet for holidaymakers coming to the coast around Swanage. It could include:

- places where they could stay
- activities they could do
- a guide to a coastal walk
- descriptions and explanations of some coastal landforms they would see on the walk.

You can use a desk-top publishing package on a computer to help you to produce the leaflet.

Design a cover page. Think of a good title. Use photographs, maps or drawings to make it colourful.

Look at map E on page 13. What places can you find to stay, in and around Swanage? List the places and show their location on a map.

Draw some of the coastal landforms that can be seen on the walk. Explain why they are there and how they have been formed. It could help to include a map of the geology.

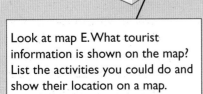

Look at map E. What tourist information is shown on the map? List the activities you could do and show their location on a map.

Describe a walk along the coast path from the Foreland to Durlston Head. Draw a map and label each section of the walk. Give grid references, distances and directions.

1.7 Cliff collapse!

In this case study you will investigate what happened when a hotel fell into the sea, and then produce your own TV report.

NORTH SEA

Scarborough • Flamborough Head

YORKSHIRE

Bridlington •

Living near the coast is meant to be good for your health. It can also be very dangerous! Occasionally, the dangers of being near the sea are headline news.

YORKSHIRE DAILY NEWS

Saturday 5th June, 1993

HOTEL FALLS INTO THE SEA

A four-star hotel was, last night, falling into the sea after a 1-km section of the cliff top at Scarborough collapsed into the sea. Holbeck Hall, which has stood overlooking the North Sea for more than a hundred years, has been gradually falling apart since the collapse began in the early hours of yesterday morning.

Eighty guests, who had each paid £100 a night to stay at the hotel, had to be woken early to evacuate the hotel. One guest commented, 'I hardly had time to pack my bags. I looked out of the window and I could see that half of the lawn had vanished. I didn't need to be persuaded to leave!' Guests were asked to settle their bills as they left, but they were not charged for breakfast. By lunchtime, half of the hotel, including its new restaurant, had disappeared over the edge of the cliff.

The destruction of the hotel was particularly surprising as it lay 100 m from the cliff edge. Michael Clements, Scarborough's director of engineering, explained: 'The fall was due to a landslip in the cliffs. They're made of clay, and after a few dry summers they begin to develop cracks. It only takes a wet winter, like the one we've just had, to let water into the cracks and then they begin to slip.' Other home owners near Holbeck Hall have expressed their concern. They want to know how safe their own properties will be. Engineers are due to begin tests on the cliff today to see if the ground is still moving. They will then have to decide on the best way to stabilise the cliffs to prevent them slipping again.

This is not the first time a building on the east coast of Yorkshire has fallen into the sea. Along the coast,

The final moments as the hotel falls into the sea

south of Flamborough Head, whole villages have been lost as a result of coastal erosion. Up to 2 m of land is lost each year in this way. A geologist from Hull University said, 'It is unusual for such a large chunk of land to disappear at one time, but we have to expect events like this to happen every now and again. We can build sea walls to try to protect the cliffs, but whatever we do the sea will continue to erode the coast. All we can do is delay it for a bit longer.'

Holbeck Hall

Sea wall

Sea

Before and after the collapse

Protecting the coast

For centuries people have tried to protect the coast from the power of the sea. Seaside towns are often protected by strong sea walls, but even these may be no match for the waves on a stormy sea. A better understanding of the geology of the coastline may help to protect the coast.

▲ **A** A sea wall at Cromer in Norfolk

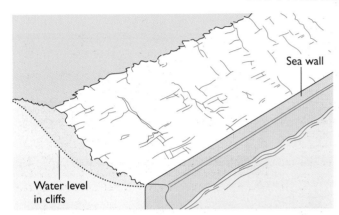

▲ **B** Cliffs can be protected by building a sea wall in front of them. The wall prevents the waves from eroding the base of the cliff. It deflects the power of the waves away from the coast and back to the sea.

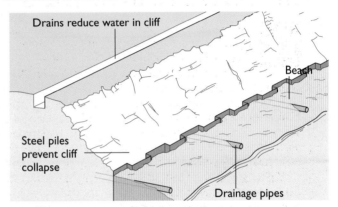

▲ **C** Cliffs can be drained to reduce the amount of water in them. Drains near the cliff top take water away before it can seep into the cliff. Steel barriers hammered into the rock near the base of the cliff collect the remaining water, which drains out through pipes.

Activities

1 Study the newspaper article on the opposite page. Which of the statements below could be used to explain why the hotel fell into the sea?

   * There was a severe storm.
   * Water had seeped into the cliff.
   * The hotel was right at the edge of the cliff.
   * The cliff had become unstable.
   * The cliff was made of hard limestone.
   * The cliff was made of soft clay.
   * The cliff had become stable.
   * There was a landslip in the cliff.
   * There is no sea wall at Scarborough.

2 Look at the two methods of protecting the coast shown in diagrams B and C. Which might be the best method to prevent further cliff collapses in the area near Holbeck Hall Hotel? Explain why this method might work.

Assignment

Work in a group of four.

Imagine that you are a TV news crew, sent to Scarborough after the hotel fell into the sea. You have been asked to find out:

   * what happened
   * why it happened
   * if it could happen again, and how people feel about that
   * how it could be prevented from happening again.

Interview these people mentioned in the newspaper article to get the answers to your questions – *the hotel owner, a nearby resident, the director of engineering, a geologist.*

   Take turns to be the interviewer and the person being interviewed. Your teacher may give you more information about your role.

1.8 How does a river change along its course?

In this case study you will use photos and maps to identify the changes that occur along the River Severn between its source and mouth.

The River Severn is the longest river in Britain. From its source in the Cambrian Mountains it flows 354 km through Wales and England until it enters the Bristol Channel close to the border between the two countries. Along its course, between source and mouth, many changes occur.

R. Severn

▲ A

▲ B

Activities

1 Look at photos A and B.
   a) Identify the river landforms in each photo (look back at pages 8–9 for ideas).
   b) Which photo was taken nearest to the source? Give a reason for your answer.

2 Study map extracts C and E. Find the River Severn on each map. Match each map with one of the two photos. Give the reasons for your choice.

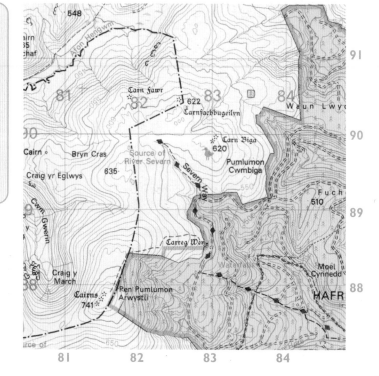

► C Map extract. Reproduced from the 2002 1:50,000 Ordnance Survey map by permission of the Controller of HMSO © Crown Copyright.

Ordnance Survey maps have **contour lines**. They are lines that join places of the same height on a map. The lines are numbered, showing the height of the land in metres. Contour lines also show us the shape of the land, or **relief**. The closer the contour lines are, the steeper the land is. If there are no contour lines the land is flat.

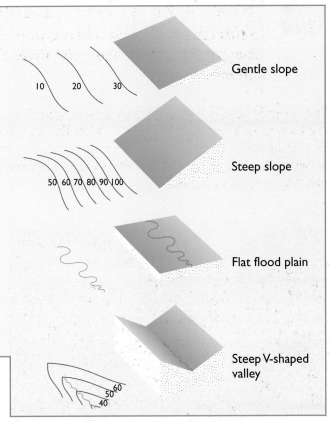

▲ **D** Contour patterns and relief

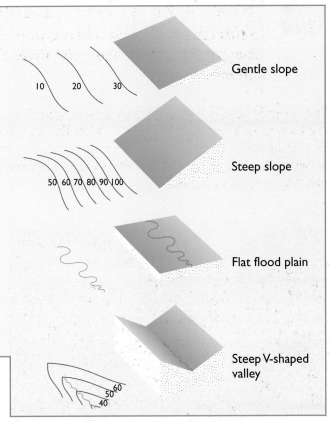

▲ **E** Map extract. Reproduced from the 2002 1:50,000 Ordnance Survey map by permission of the Controller of HMSO © Crown Copyright.

3 Study the information in box D. It shows how the relief, or shape of the land, is drawn as contours on an OS map.
   Find these squares on each map:
   i)   8289 on map C   ii)   0391 on map E.
   Describe the landscape that you find in each square.

4 Below is a simple sketch map of C.
   a) On a large copy of the sketch map label the following features:
   - the source of the River Severn
   - the river valley
   - a waterfall
   - a steep valley side
   - a forest.

   b) Draw a sketch map of E. On your map label:
   - the River Severn
   - the flood plain
   - steep land
   - main roads
   - the village of Caersws.

How do human activities change along the river?

▲ **F** Llyn Clewedog reservoir

▲ **G** Aerial view showing Shrewsbury on the River Severn

▲ **H** The Severn Bridge

Like many rivers, the River Severn has always played an important role in people's lives. Settlements grew up along the river because it provided a convenient water supply and means of human transport. Some settlements were built at bridging points where the river could easily be crossed. Others, like Shrewsbury, were built on meanders that provided a natural defence for the settlement. In the eighteenth century, the River Severn became a source of power for the new iron-working industries at the beginning of the Industrial Revolution. Ironbridge was the site of the world's first metal bridge, built with locally made iron. The Severn was also a convenient means of transport for the new industrial goods, and ports grew along the river as far upstream as Welshpool, where the water was deep enough for boats to navigate.

Today, the River Severn still plays an important part in people's lives, although the locations of many activities have changed. The river is still a major source of water. Much of it is collected in reservoirs high in the Cambrian Mountains and then piped to the areas where it is needed – particularly to the West Midlands. The lowest bridging point on the river is the Severn Bridge – linking England and Wales on the M4 motorway. Ports too have moved downstream as boats have increased in size. The largest port is Avonmouth on the Severn estuary, where the river widens to meet the Bristol Channel.

Activities

I Look at photos F–H. Locate each of the places on map I.

   On which part of the River Severn was each photo taken – the upper, middle or lower course?

2 Identify the human activities that you can see in each photo on this page. Write a sentence about each activity to explain why this is a good location for it.

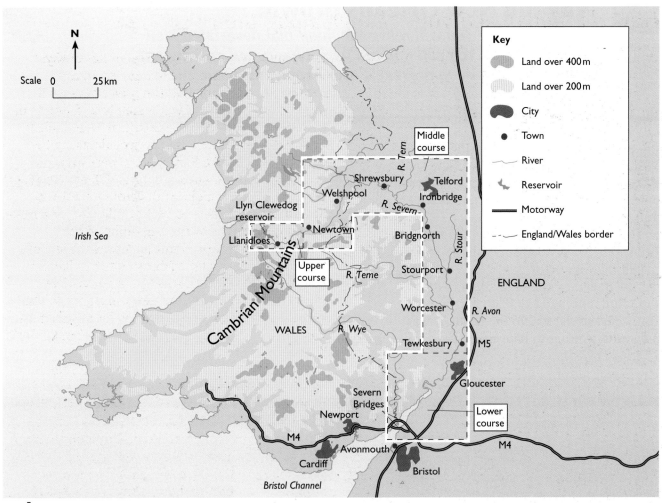

▲ I The course of the River Severn. The river can be divided into three sections – the upper course, the middle course and the lower course. In each of these sections the river and its valley will have different features. Human activities also change along the course of the river.

Assignment

Copy and complete a large table, like the one below, to compare the upper, middle and lower course of the River Severn. Use all the photos and maps on pages 18–21 to help you describe each section of the river. The information on pages 8–9 will also help.

Section of the river	River channel		What landforms are there?	What processes are at work?	What shape is the valley?	What tributaries flow into the river?	What towns and cities are there?	What activities happen here?
	How wide is the channel?	How straight or bendy is it?						
Upper course								

1.9   Why did New Orleans drown?

In this case study you will relive the flood that devastated New Orleans in 2005. You will find out why it happened and suggest what could be done to prevent it ever happening again.

On 29 August 2005, Hurricane Katrina hit New Orleans. The storm led to one of the worst floods ever to affect the USA. Within two days, 80 per cent of New Orleans had been flooded, over a million people had been evacuated from the city, and almost 1,300 people died.

Yet, nobody could say they had not been warned. New Orleans is built on a marsh that lies below sea level. The city is surrounded by the Mississippi River to the south, and by Lake Pontchartrain, connected to the sea, to the north. It was a disaster waiting to happen.

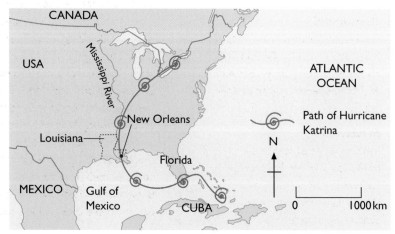

▲ **A** The path of Hurricane Katrina

▲ **B** New Orleans under water

Diary of a Disaster

Tuesday 23 August

US National Hurricane Centre warns of a tropical storm over the Atlantic Ocean.

Thursday 25

The tropical storm grows into a hurricane as it hits Florida. It is named Katrina. Nine people die and the power supply to millions is cut off.

Sunday 28

Katrina gains strength over the Gulf of Mexico with winds reaching 160 km per hour. The Mayor of New Orleans orders the city to be evacuated. Roads out of the city are gridlocked. Many are unable to escape. Thousands of people take shelter in the Superdome – an indoor stadium in the middle of the city.

Monday 29

Katrina hits land south of New Orleans at 6a.m. It brings hurricane force winds and torrential rain. Floodwater soon starts to rise and people are forced onto their roofs. Bodies are seen floating in the streets.

Tuesday 30

Four **levees** – the flood banks that protect the city from the lake and the river – are breached by water, having been damaged by the storm. More water pours into the city. Water levels continue to rise.

Wednesday 31

Eighty per cent of the city is under water. Thousands of people are made homeless. There is looting and shooting as desperate people steal food and cars in which to escape. The State Governor orders everyone to leave the city. Rescue helicopters pick up survivors and buses take people to other cities in the USA.

One family's story

Robert Green lost two members of his family in the dark morning hours on the day Katrina hit New Orleans. A barge crashed though the floodwall on the Intracoastal Canal three blocks away from their house. It sent a 6-m wave of water into the neighbourhood, ripping homes from their foundations.

As water chased them into the attic, Robert and his brother kicked a hole in the roof, dragging their 73-year-old mother and three granddaughters with them. The raging waters soon shredded the wooden house. To escape, they scrambled from rooftop to rooftop. Robert's mother and one of the girls, Shenae, fell into the flood. Shenae never resurfaced. The brothers managed to pull their mother up and resuscitate her, but she later died. They left their mother's body lying on a rooftop to concentrate on saving the rest of the family.

Two months later Robert identified Shenae's body at the city morgue, but there was no sign of his mother's body. It was four months later that Robert and his brother were finally allowed back into the neighbourhood to search for their mother. They found her clothes and skeleton just a few metres from the house where they had left her. At last, they were able to bury her.

▲ **C** Many people were rescued from their rooftops by helicopter

Activities

I Study all the information on this spread. Imagine that you were living in New Orleans. How would you have tried to survive Katrina?

   a) Would you have tried to escape from the city? If so, how and when?

   b) Or, would you have stayed? If so, where and why? What would you have needed in order to survive?

2 Do you think that a flood like this could ever affect the city that you live in (or your nearest city)? Give reasons for your answer.

Was the flood a natural or man-made disaster?

New Orleans has always been at risk from flooding. The original settlement was built just above sea level, protected from seasonal river floods by levees. During the twentieth century the city expanded onto the surrounding marshland and the levees were built higher. In 1965 Hurricane Betsy led to severe flooding, so flood defences were further improved. Even so, in 2001 the *Houston Chronicle* predicted that, if a severe hurricane were to hit New Orleans, the city would drown and people would die. Unfortunately, they were right.

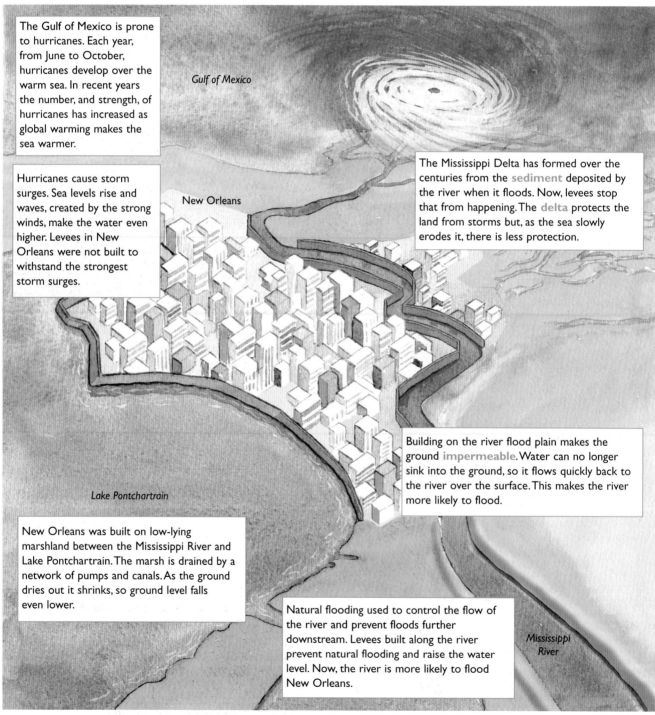

The Gulf of Mexico is prone to hurricanes. Each year, from June to October, hurricanes develop over the warm sea. In recent years the number, and strength, of hurricanes has increased as global warming makes the sea warmer.

Hurricanes cause storm surges. Sea levels rise and waves, created by the strong winds, make the water even higher. Levees in New Orleans were not built to withstand the strongest storm surges.

The Mississippi Delta has formed over the centuries from the sediment deposited by the river when it floods. Now, levees stop that from happening. The delta protects the land from storms but, as the sea slowly erodes it, there is less protection.

Building on the river flood plain makes the ground impermeable. Water can no longer sink into the ground, so it flows quickly back to the river over the surface. This makes the river more likely to flood.

New Orleans was built on low-lying marshland between the Mississippi River and Lake Pontchartrain. The marsh is drained by a network of pumps and canals. As the ground dries out it shrinks, so ground level falls even lower.

Natural flooding used to control the flow of the river and prevent floods further downstream. Levees built along the river prevent natural flooding and raise the water level. Now, the river is more likely to flood New Orleans.

Gulf of Mexico

New Orleans

Lake Pontchartrain

Mississippi River

▲ **D** Causes of flooding in New Orleans

NEW ORLEANS

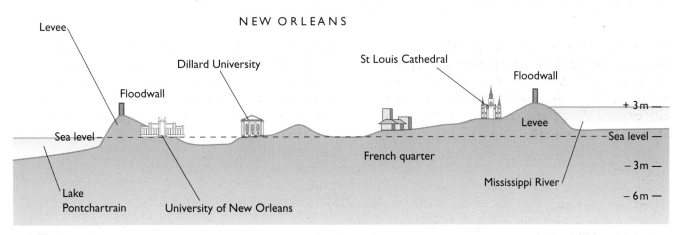

▲ **E** Cross-section of New Orleans

Before Katrina, there was concern that the levees along the river and canals were not designed to cope with the strongest hurricanes. Although Katrina was only a category 3 hurricane (on a scale from 1 to 5), it passed very slowly over New Orleans. This gave time for the wind and rain to do their damage. Levees were breached at four points in the city (photo E).

▶ **F** A breach in one of the levees in New Orleans

Activities

1 Look at drawing D. Complete a large copy of the map below, to show the location of New Orleans. Colour and label the following features on the map:

> New Orleans   Mississippi River
> Lake Pontchartrain   Gulf of Mexico
> Mississippi Delta

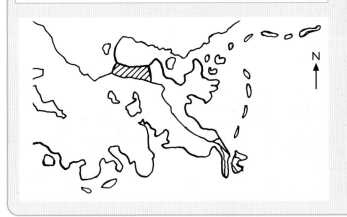

2 Study the information on drawing D. Find all the causes of flooding in New Orleans, both physical and human.

a) Make a large table, like the one below, to list all the physical and human causes of flooding. The first two are done for you.

Physical causes	Human causes
Hurricane Katrina	Global warming (due to burning fossil fuels) could be making hurricanes stronger and more frequent

b) Study your table. On balance, do you think the flood was a natural or a man-made disaster? Give the most important reason.

3 Look carefully at drawing D and cross-section E.

a) Where was the flooding caused by Hurricane Katrina most likely to come from – Lake Pontchartrain or the Mississippi River?

b) Give reasons for your answer.

Could another disaster be avoided?

Flooding is a natural hazard. It is difficult to avoid. Floods are caused by rivers overflowing their banks, or by sea level rising higher than the coastline. New Orleans, lying between the Mississippi River and Lake Pontchartrain, faces both dangers. In the August 2005 hurricane the flood was caused by a storm surge that caused water level in the lake to rise.

Not all natural hazards lead to disasters. Disasters happen when people are not properly prepared. Sometimes, human actions can make the hazard worse. In New Orleans, both of these things happened.

▼ **H** Map of New Orleans

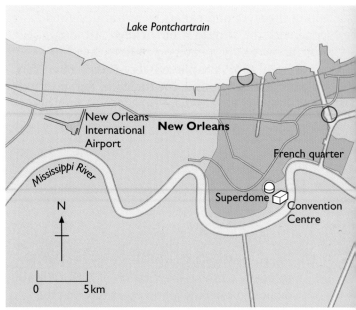

▲ **G** satellite image of New Orleans on 31 August 2005. Water appears green in the photo. Dry areas are brown.

Activities

1 Look at satellite image G. Compare it with map H.
   a) Shade the areas that were flooded onto an outline of the photo.
   b) What evidence can you find that the floodwater came from Lake Pontchartrain, and not the Mississippi?
   c) Why were the Superdome and Convention Centre both used to accommodate homeless people?

▲ I A flooded highway

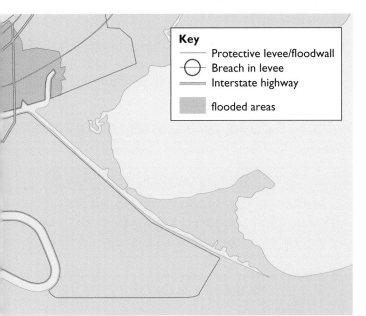

Key
—⊙— Protective levee/floodwall
—⊙— Breach in levee
═══ Interstate highway
▨ flooded areas

What turned a hazard into a disaster?

- The Mayor of New Orleans did not call for the city to be evacuated until 28 August, less than 24 hours before Katrina hit the city.

- The roads were gridlocked so it was impossible for some people to escape in their cars.

- Many poor people in New Orleans have no car, and there are not many buses.

- 25,000 people crowded into the Superdome and another 20,000 into the Convention Centre (map H). The buildings became overheated and unhealthy. Some people died.

- With most roads flooded (photo I), it took three days to organise enough helicopters to evacuate people trapped by the floods.

- Shops were closed and water supplies were contaminated, so many people did not have enough to eat or drink. Some people looted shops to get what they needed.

- Many police had evacuated from the city before the flood. There were not enough left to keep law and order in the city.

- Dead bodies were left floating in water for days, which was upsetting and unhealthy.

Assignment

You are the new Mayor of New Orleans. You have to produce a Flood Action Plan to reduce the danger of any future floods in New Orleans and prevent another disaster. Divide your plan into two sections:

- *What to do now*
  What can you do to reduce the chance of another flood happening in future? Use the ideas that you studied on pages 24–25.
- *What to do before, during and after a flood*
  What can you do to prevent a flood turning into a disaster, as it did in August 2005? Use the ideas on pages 22–23 and on this spread. What would you do better?

▲ J A desperate mother waiting to be evacuated from the Convention Centre

TEST YOURSELF

I Choose the correct meaning for weathering and erosion.
- wearing away of the land
- the breakdown of rocks

2 Name three agents – or causes – of erosion in the natural landscape.

3 Label the three coastal landforms that you can see in this drawing.

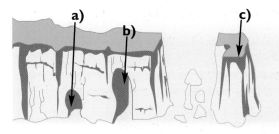

a)   b)   c)

4 Write three sentences to describe how the landforms in Question 3 were formed.

5 Name three jobs that rivers do to help them shape the land.

6 a) Complete this drawing of a waterfall. Label: soft rock, hard rock, plunge pool.
b) Now, draw what the waterfall may look like many years from now. Annotate the drawing to show how the waterfall has changed.

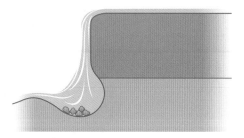

7 a) What is a glacier?
b) Name two landforms made by glaciers.
c) In which part of Britain are you most likely to find glacial landforms? Why?
d) Name two parts of the world where you could find glaciers today.

8 Which is the odd one out in these groups of words? In each case, explain why.
a) river   valley   glacier   sea
b) transportation   erosion   source   deposition
c) flood plain   waterfall   V-shaped valley   gorge
d) U-shaped valley   beach   cliff   spit

NOW, FOR A CHALLENGE!

9 How do rivers or the sea change the shape of the land?

Write a paragraph to describe the ways in which either a river or the sea has changed the shape of the land. Include the names of landforms you have studied.

10 Flooding is a natural hazard – agree or disagree? Answer this question, referring to the 2005 flood in New Orleans, or another recent flood you have studied.

These are the words you should try to learn for this unit:

TOP TEN WORDS

weathering   erosion   transportation
deposition   coast   cliff   beach
valley   waterfall   glacier

MORE KEY WORDS

landform   bay   headland
cave   arch   stack   spit
V-shaped valley   meander
gorge   flood plain   plunge pool
ice sheet   U-shaped valley
cirque   moraine   longshore drift

IMPRESS YOUR TEACHER!

physical weathering
chemical weathering
biological weathering   process
geology   alluvium   sediment
sedimentary rock   impermeable
terminal moraine   levee

UNIT 2

Weather and Climate

◀ A tornado in the Bristol Channel on 11 June 2004

Fortunately, we don't get this sort of weather too often. Weather is the condition of the atmosphere, or air around us, from day to day.

- At what time of year do you think the photo was taken?
- How can you tell?
- What do you expect the weather to be like at this time of year?
- Why is weather so unpredictable?

2.1 Here is the weather forecast ...

▲ **A** A weather satellite in orbit around the Earth

Every day, on the TV and on radio, you can hear the weather forecast. It tells you what the weather will be like for the next few days. In the UK weather forecasting is difficult because the weather changes so much from day to day.

People who study the weather are called meteorologists. In Britain our weather forecasts come from the Meteorological Office (or Met. Office for short). Nowadays meteorology is very scientific. All around the country, from the Scilly Isles to Shetland, weather observations are taken every hour. These are backed up by hundreds of other observations taken out at sea, and by weather balloons in the air and weather satellites in space. Computers build up a picture of the weather from all this information. This is used by skilled meteorologists to make their forecasts.

Activities

1 Look at map B. Can you recognise all the symbols on the weather map?
2 Write a short script for the weather forecaster in B to read, to give the weather forecast shown on the map. Mention each part of the country in your script.

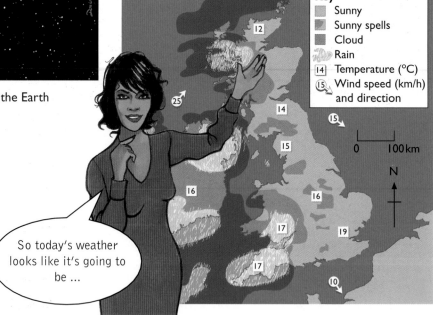

So today's weather looks like it's going to be ...

▲ **B** A TV weather forecast

We all depend on the weather forecast, even if only to help us decide what to wear. With the help of modern technology, weather forecasts today are usually quite accurate. This is important to those people whose jobs, or even whose safety, can be affected by the weather.

◀ **C** Fishing in the North Sea

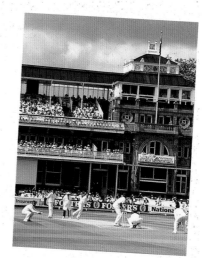

▲ **D** Cricket at Lord's, in London

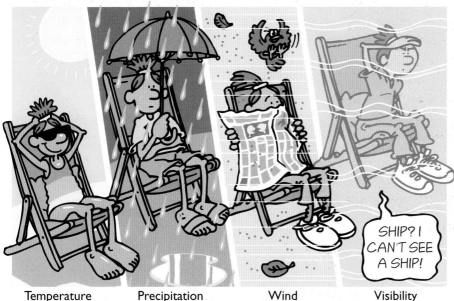

SHIP? I CAN'T SEE A SHIP!

Temperature   Precipitation   Wind   Visibility

▲ **E** Important elements of the weather

▲ **F** Selling ice creams at Blackpool

---

3 Match each element of the weather in drawing E with the correct meaning below.

- Movement of the air
- Water in the air that falls to the ground as rain, snow, sleet or hail
- A measure of how hot or cold the air is
- The distance through the air that you can see.

Write each word with the correct meaning beside it.

4 Look at the photos C, D and F.

  a) Explain how the people in each photo would be affected by the weather. Which element of the weather would most affect the people in each photo?

  b) Find a map of Britain in your atlas. Locate where the people in each photo are working. How would they be affected by the weather shown on map B?

  c) Think of other people whose jobs could be affected by the weather. Make a list.

Homework

5 How accurate is the weather forecast? Listen to the TV or radio weather forecast. Make a note of the main points in the forecast. Compare the forecast with the weather the following day in your own area. How much of the forecast was correct? Did they get anything wrong?

2.2   **Weather check**

You do not need to have computers and satellites to forecast the weather – although they certainly help! The most important thing is to be able to observe the weather around you, and to record what you find. Most weather observation is carried out at weather stations. A weather station is a collection of instruments that are kept in an open area, away from buildings and trees. Your school might be lucky enough to have its own weather station.

Stevenson Screen
A box made from wooden slats, which stands on legs above the ground. The slats allow air to circulate around the box without direct sunlight reaching the instruments, which are kept inside.

Maximum/minimum thermometer
A U-shaped thermometer with two scales to record the highest and lowest temperature each day. Columns of liquid inside the thermometer push two small pins up the tube as temperature changes. At the end of each day the pins are reset.

Rain gauge
A cylinder set into the ground to catch the rain as it falls. The rainwater is funnelled into a measuring container. The level of the water is read each day before the container is emptied.

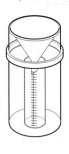

Wind sock
A large nylon sock mounted on a pole. Wind blows into the sock and turns it in the direction of the wind. The pointer then shows where the wind is blowing from.

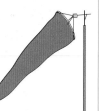

Anemometer
Three metal cups mounted on a high pole. As the wind blows it makes the cups spin. The wind speed is shown on a dial below, rather like a car speedometer.

Barometer
Mercury inside the barometer changes level as air pressure goes up or down. The higher the pressure the greater the weight of mercury it can support. The dial on the barometer reads the air pressure.

Mirror
A mirror, divided into squares, is placed on the ground where it can reflect the sky. The number of squares covered by clouds shows what proportion of the sky has cloud cover.

Temperature

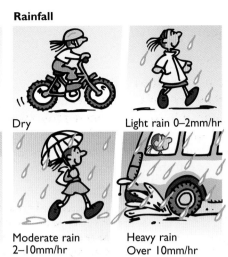

Freezing Below 0°C   Cold 0–15°C

Warm 15–30°C   Hot Over 30°C

Rainfall

Dry   Light rain 0–2mm/hr

Moderate rain
2–10mm/hr   Heavy rain
Over 10mm/hr

Cloud cover

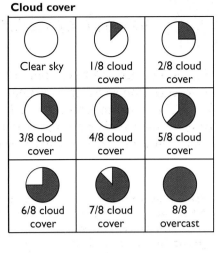

Clear sky	1/8 cloud cover	2/8 cloud cover
3/8 cloud cover	4/8 cloud cover	5/8 cloud cover
6/8 cloud cover	7/8 cloud cover	8/8 overcast

Wind speed (Beaufort Scale)

| Calm
0–3km/hr | Light breeze
4–15km/hr | Moderate breeze
16–35km/hr | Strong breeze
36–56km/hr | Gale
57–90km/hr | Storm
91–120km/hr |

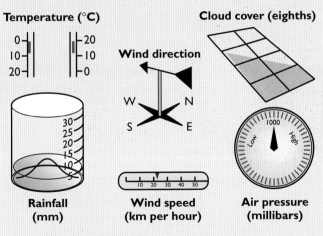

Activities

1 Study the information about a weather station on the opposite page. List the instruments, and what each one is used to measure.

2 On a day in April the instruments at a weather station showed the measurements that you can see in the box below.

Temperature (°C)

0 –|
10 –| |– 20
20 –| |– 10
            |– 0

Cloud cover (eighths)

Wind direction

W   N
S   E

**Rainfall
(mm)**

**Wind speed
(km per hour)**

**Air pressure
(millibars)**

a) Write down each of the measurements.

b) What words could you use to describe the weather that day?

c) Think of words to describe the weather in your local area today.

Homework

3 Observe and record the weather in your area for a week. Do this at the same time each day at your school weather station. If you don't have a weather station, use newspaper weather reports and the words on this page to record the weather each day.

   Record your observations in a table like the one below. Draw graphs to show temperature and rainfall. Use a line graph to record temperature and a bar graph to record rainfall.

	Mon	Tues	Wed	Thur	Fri	Sat	Sun
Date							
Temperature (°C)	X X						
Rainfall (mm)							
Wind direction	W						
Wind speed (km/hr)	22						
Cloud cover (1/8s)	4/8						
Air pressure (mb)	1,000						

2.3   Microclimates

Weather and climate can vary within a small area. They can vary even from one side of a building to another.

Have you noticed that some classrooms in your school are much sunnier? Do you find that some parts of the playground get more wet and windy? Local variations in climate like these are known as microclimates. Some of the reasons for different microclimates are shown around photo A.

Ground surface can influence the local climate. Dark, artificial surfaces, like tarmac, warm up faster and give off more heat than light, natural surfaces, like grass.

Walls, buildings and trees provide shelter from wind. Places that are sheltered may also feel warmer and get less rain.

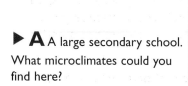

▶**A** A large secondary school. What microclimates could you find here?

Wind direction

Aspect is the direction in which a place faces. Places that face the sun are warmer than those in shadow. In the UK places with a south-facing aspect get more sun and higher temperatures.

Buildings can change the wind speed and direction, creating some areas of calm and other areas that are windy. On warm, sunny days buildings absorb heat and, later, give it off. Night-time temperatures in cities can be 2–3°C warmer than surrounding areas.

Activities

1 Look at photo A and the information around it.

a) Find places 1 and 2 on the photo. Notice the compass and wind direction.
   Which place is likely to be:
   i) sunniest   iii) windiest
   ii) warmest   iv) wettest?

b) Give reasons for each of your answers.

2 Do the same activity for your own school grounds based on personal experience. Think of a place that is:
   i) sunny   iii) windy
   ii) warm   iv) wet.
   Give reasons for each one. You can check your ideas later when you carry out a microclimate investigation around the school.

3 a) Draw a simple sketch of the tree at the centre of photo A and the position of the shadow, like this:

Add a compass to your drawing. What do you think was the position of the sun in the sky when the photo was taken? What time do you think it was?

b) Now draw the position of the tree's shadow:
   i) early in the morning
   ii) late in the afternoon.

c) How is the microclimate at place 1 on photo A likely to change during the day? Use your sketch to help you to explain your answer.

Local investigation

You have to choose the best site for a new lunchtime picnic area in your school grounds. First, you will need to carry out a microclimate survey. Your teacher will divide the class into groups. Each group will record the microclimate at different sites around the school.

Each group will need:
• a plan of the school with the sites marked on it
• a recording sheet and clipboard
• a thermometer
• a compass.

Record your results at each site in a table like the one shown below:
• Write down the type of ground surface.
• Record the temperature using a thermometer. The best type to use is a digital thermometer that will give a quick reading. Otherwise you need to allow a few minutes to get a reliable reading.
• Record the wind direction using a compass. Hold the compass horizontal so that the needle points

North. Then find the wind direction. (Important: wind direction is the direction the wind blows from, **not** the direction it blows to.)
• Record the wind speed. The only accurate way to do this is with a hand-held anemometer. If you do not have one, use one of these words to describe wind speed.

Strong – hard to hold the clipboard still in the wind
Moderate – paper on the clipboard blows away if you let go (do not lose your recording sheet!)
Light – paper rustles in the wind, but does not blow away
Still – no wind at all

Back in the classroom, share your results with the rest of your class. Complete the recording sheet for all the sites on the school plan.

Finally, decide which would be the best site for a new lunchtime picnic area. Mark it on your plan. Write a paragraph to explain the choice you have made.

Site	Ground surface	Temperature °C	Wind direction	Wind speed (distance in metres)

2.4 Rainfall and the water cycle

We are surrounded by water – in the sea, in rivers and lakes, underground, in living things and in the air. This water is constantly moving from one water store to another. As it moves, it may change from liquid water into a solid (snow or ice) or a vapour, or back again. However, the total amount of water on the Earth stays the same. It moves around in a never-ending cycle called the water cycle.

By far the greatest volume of water is stored in the oceans – about 97 per cent of all the world's water. The rest is fresh water, and most of this is stored in the polar ice caps. Only 0.35 per cent of the world's water is found in the atmosphere at any one time, mostly in the form of water vapour (which is an invisible gas). It is this water that is responsible for giving us many different types of weather: clouds, rain, snow, hail and fog.

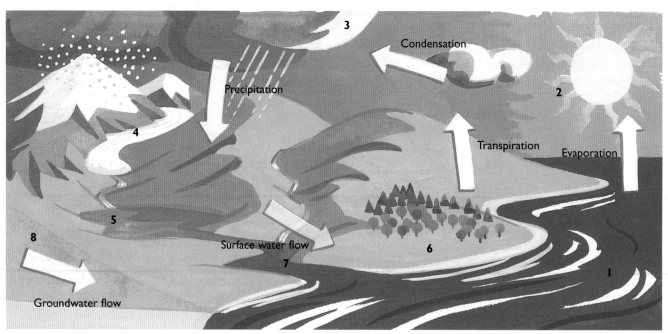

▲ **A** The water cycle

Activities

1 Look at diagram A, which shows the water cycle.
   a) Match each of the numbers with one of the places, listed in the box below, where water is stored.

clouds	groundwater	ocean	plants	lake
	glacier	river	atmosphere	

   b) Draw your own diagram of the water cycle. Label each place where water is stored on your diagram, using one of the labels from the box in place of the numbers.
   c) In each place add a label to say whether the water is stored as a liquid, a solid (ice) or as water vapour.

2 The arrows on the diagram show six ways in which water is transferred in the water cycle.
   a) Match each arrow with one of the descriptions in the box below.

   1   Water turns into vapour when heated by the sun
   2   Water vapour goes from plants into the atmosphere
   3   Water vapour rises and cools, turning into clouds
   4   Water droplets in clouds fall as rain, snow, hail or sleet
   5   Water flows over the surface of the land back to the sea
   6   Water flows through the ground

   b) Number the arrows correctly and write the descriptions in a key.

Clouds form when moist air rises and cools. Water vapour in the air condenses into tiny droplets. These droplets get bigger and heavier, until eventually they fall as rain.

Air is made to rise in three ways. Each of these ways produces a different type of rainfall.

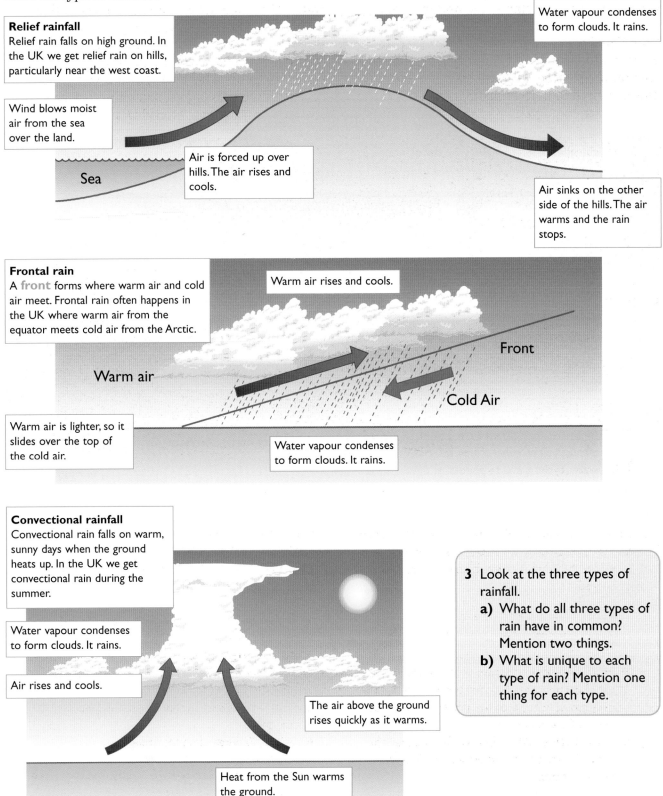

Relief rainfall
Relief rain falls on high ground. In the UK we get relief rain on hills, particularly near the west coast.

Water vapour condenses to form clouds. It rains.

Wind blows moist air from the sea over the land.

Air is forced up over hills. The air rises and cools.

Sea

Air sinks on the other side of the hills. The air warms and the rain stops.

Frontal rain
A **front** forms where warm air and cold air meet. Frontal rain often happens in the UK where warm air from the equator meets cold air from the Arctic.

Warm air rises and cools.

Front

Warm air

Cold Air

Warm air is lighter, so it slides over the top of the cold air.

Water vapour condenses to form clouds. It rains.

Convectional rainfall
Convectional rain falls on warm, sunny days when the ground heats up. In the UK we get convectional rain during the summer.

Water vapour condenses to form clouds. It rains.

Air rises and cools.

The air above the ground rises quickly as it warms.

Heat from the Sun warms the ground.

3 Look at the three types of rainfall.
  a) What do all three types of rain have in common? Mention two things.
  b) What is unique to each type of rain? Mention one thing for each type.

2.5

How does the water cycle work?

*In this game you will find out how
water moves around the water cycle.*

Activities

1 Play the Water Cycle Game on the opposite page. You
could play the game by yourself, or in a small group. If
you play in a group, each player will need a copy of the
game.

You will need: a copy of the game, a dice, scissors, card.

Before the game

Cut out eight labels, one for each of the places where
water is stored in the water cycle. Write a name on
each label (use diagram A on page 36 to help you), and
place it on the correct water store. One has been done
as an example.

Cut out twelve arrows, one for each transfer in
the water cycle. Leave the arrows blank until you play
the game.

Use a small token to play the game. This will represent
a water molecule. Place it on the ocean ready to start
the game.

Play the game

The object of the game is to visit each of the water stores
in the water cycle and to complete the labels on each of
the arrows.

Start the game. Each player takes a turn to roll the
dice. The number on each arrow on the game shows what
number you must roll to move in that direction. For
example, you must roll a one to get out of the ocean. If
you don't roll the number you need, you must wait until
your next turn to try again.

As you move your molecule, describe how the water
transfers from one store to the next. For example, as you
move from the ocean you would say, 'Water evaporates
from the ocean into the atmosphere.' Write the
description onto an arrow. Place it on the correct arrow
on the gameboard.

The game is finished when each player has visited all
the water stores at least once. Each arrow should be
labelled and placed on the game to show that you have
been all around the water cycle.

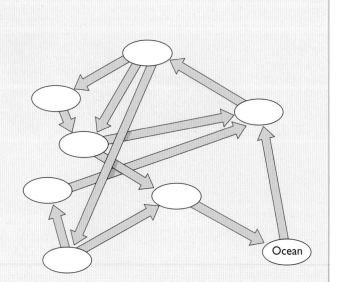

2 Write an account of what happened to your water
molecule during the Water Cycle Game. Name all the
water stores that it visited. Describe how water
transferred from one store to the next. You could start
like this:

> The water molecule began in the ocean. This is
> where most of the world's water is stored. It spent a
> long time in the ocean before it evaporated into the
> air. In the air, it was in the form of water vapour.
> Next …

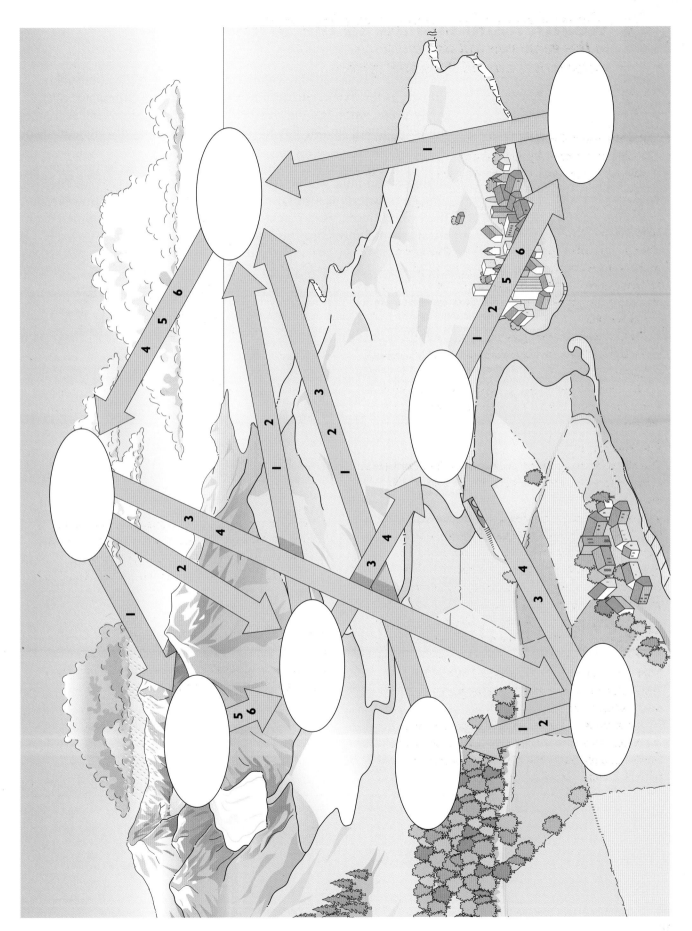

2.6   Weather and climate in the British Isles

I DON'T REMEMBER IT BEING THIS NICE LAST SUMMER!

Weather is the day-to-day conditions that exist in the atmosphere. Climate is the average pattern of weather that we experience over many years. Although the weather in the British Isles is quite unpredictable from one day to the next, climate hardly changes from year to year.

Britain has a temperate climate – that is, a climate with warm summers and mild winters. It is rarely very hot or very cold. The climate in Britain is also fairly wet throughout the year. However, there are differences in climate between one place and another, even within a small area like the British Isles.

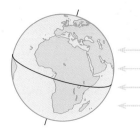

1. Distance from the equator (latitude)
Areas close to the equator are hot because the sun is directly overhead during the day. Away from the equator the sun is at a lower angle in the sky and gives less heat. The angle of the sun in the sky changes with the time of year. This is why summer is warmer than winter.

3. Distance from the sea
Land warms up and cools down more quickly than the sea. Places that are further inland become hotter in summer, but colder in winter. It is cooler near the sea in summer.

N

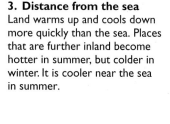

2. Height (altitude)
The higher you go in the atmosphere the colder it gets. Temperature falls 1°C for every 150 m in height.

4. Wind direction
Wind often changes direction. Winds blowing from the north in the British Isles bring cold air. Winds from the south bring warmer air. The prevailing wind in Britain is from the south-west. This brings warm moist air from the Atlantic Ocean.

S

▲ **A** Reasons for differences in temperature

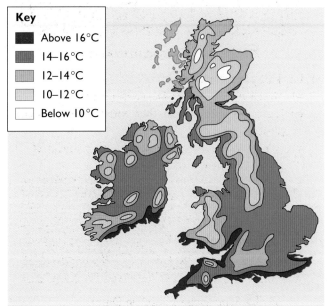

Key
- ■ Above 16°C
- ■ 14–16°C
- ■ 12–14°C
- ■ 10–12°C
- □ Below 10°C

▲ **B** Summer – July average temperature

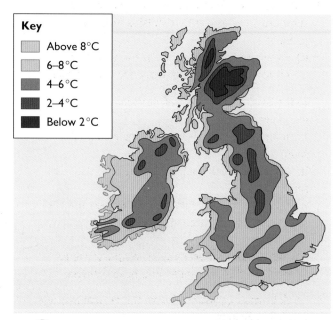

Key
- □ Above 8°C
- ■ 6–8°C
- ■ 4–6°C
- ■ 2–4°C
- ■ Below 2°C

▲ **C** Winter – January average temperature

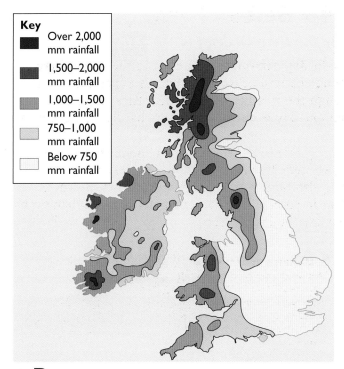

Key
- ■ Over 2,000 mm rainfall
- ■ 1,500–2,000 mm rainfall
- ■ 1,000–1,500 mm rainfall
- ■ 750–1,000 mm rainfall
- □ Below 750 mm rainfall

▲ **D** Annual average rainfall

Key
- ■ Land over 200 m

A

Prevailing wind

B

▲ **E** Relief (height of the land)

Activities

1 Read the phrases in the box below. Is each one referring to the weather or the climate, do you think?

> sunny spells   average annual rainfall
> thundery showers   overnight frost
> hot summers   an unusually wet autumn

2 Look at maps B and C, which show average temperatures in the British Isles in July and January.

a) Re-write the sentences in the box below, choosing the correct word from each pair.

> In the British Isles it is warmer/cooler in July than in January.
> In summer the north is warmer/cooler than the south.
> In winter the north-east is milder/colder than the south-west.
> In summer and winter the lowest temperatures are found on high land/around the coast.

b) Explain the differences in temperature for each of the sentences you have written.

3 Look at map D, which shows the annual average rainfall in Britain.

a) Describe the rainfall pattern in your own words. The sentences in 2 will give you ideas.

b) Compare map D with map E, which shows the height of the land. Describe the link that you can see.

▲ **F** Winter in the Scottish mountains

4 Look at photos F and G.

a) Match these places with A and B on map E.

b) Describe the weather that you can see in each photo.

c) Is it typical at this time of year, do you think? Give reasons for your answers.

▲ **G** Summer on a beach in Devon

2.7

Why is the Lake District so wet?

In this case study you will find out why the Lake District is so wet, and how an understanding of the weather can improve safety in the mountains.

I live in one of the wettest parts of the British Isles, in the Lake District. In an average year it rains here for 200 days out of 365, and the annual rainfall is over three times that of London. But there are plenty of good reasons to live here, despite the weather. It's one of the most beautiful areas I know. People come in their thousands to enjoy the lakes and the mountains here. If it didn't rain so much it wouldn't look so green!

Hilary is a volunteer with the mountain rescue service in the Lake District

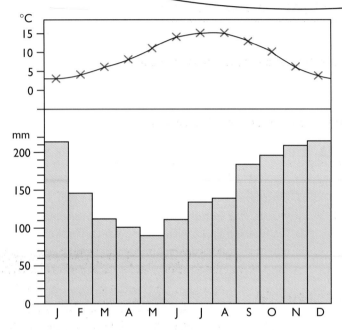

◀ **A** Temperature and rainfall graphs for Ambleside, in the Lake District

▲ **B** Walkers in the Lake District

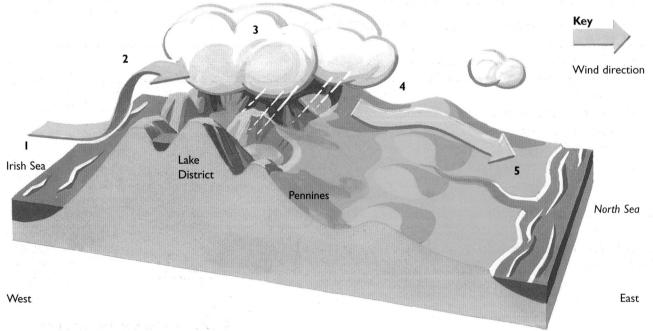

Key

Wind direction

West

Irish Sea

Lake District

Pennines

North Sea

East

▲ **C** Relief rainfall in the Lake District

Activities

1 Look at A, which shows temperature and rainfall graphs for Ambleside, in the Lake District.
   a) What is the average July temperature? What is the average January temperature?
   b) Work out the annual average rainfall. Add the monthly rainfall totals.

2 Look at the table below, which shows the monthly average temperature and rainfall in London.

	J	F	M	A	M	J	J	A	S	O	N	D
Temperature (°C)	4	5	7	10	13	16	18	17	15	11	8	6
Rainfall (mm)	54	40	37	37	46	45	57	59	49	57	64	48

   a) Draw temperature and rainfall graphs for London.
   b) Compare the temperature and rainfall in London and the Lake District. What are the similarities? What are the differences?

3 Look at diagram C.
   a) Match each of the labels in the box below with one of the numbers on the diagram.

> • Air sinks on the other side of the hills. The air warms and the rain stops.
> • Wind blows moist air from the sea over the land
> • Low land to the east of the hills receives little rain. This is a rain shadow.
> • Air is forced up over hills. The air rises and cools.
> • Water vapour condenses to form clouds. It rains.

   b) Write the sentences in the correct order to describe how relief rainfall happens.
   c) What is meant by the term 'rain shadow'.

4 Study weather warning D, then answer these questions.
   a) What is the date?
   b) What is the weather forecast for the day?
   c) How does this compare with the average December weather in graph A?
   d) What happens to the temperature as you go higher?
   e) You are planning a walk in the Lake District up to 600 metres. Would you go ahead with your planned walk after reading this forecast? Give reasons for your decision.

Hilary is often called out to help people in trouble on the mountains when the weather suddenly gets worse. To reduce the danger, weather warnings are given for people thinking of climbing (D).

Lake District National Park Authority

W E A T H E R   F O R E C A S T

Specially prepared by the Meteorological Office, Newcastle-on-Tyne with fell conditions from November to Easter provided by the Lake District National Park Authority

DATE: *20 DEC 2006*   SUNRISE: *8 : 22*   SUNSET: *15 : 51*

GENERAL REMARKS:

CLOUDY

PATCHY RAIN OR DRIZZLE LATER

WIND: *MODERATE TO FRESH, NORTH WESTERLY FRESH TO STRONG ON FELL TOPS*

TEMPERATURE: *+9° C - +4° C AT 3000 FEET*

CLOUD: *BASE 1000 FEET*

VISIBILITY: *POOR ABOVE 1000 FEET*

FELL CONDITIONS: Please keep your dog on a lead near sheep, and under control at all times.

VERY WET AND MUDDY ON PATHS. NO ICE

HAWKSHEAD
Supports the
Lake District National Park Weatherline
*Great clothing
-whatever the weather.*

Lake District National Park
WEATHERLINE
017687 75757
12 Lines – 24 Hour Service
All calls at normal rates
updated at 08.00 & 17.30

▲ **D** A weather warning in the Lake District

Will it be safe on the mountain?

Changeable! That is one word to describe the weather in the Lake District. It can be sunny in the morning and raining by lunchtime. On the hilltops you can suddenly be caught in a blizzard or lost in cloud. That's why it is so important to listen to the weather forecast before you start walking.

One of the main reasons for our changeable weather in the British Isles is depressions. A depression is a large area of low pressure that develops where warm air and cold air meet at a front. The warm air rises over the cold air, bringing cloud and rain (see page 37).

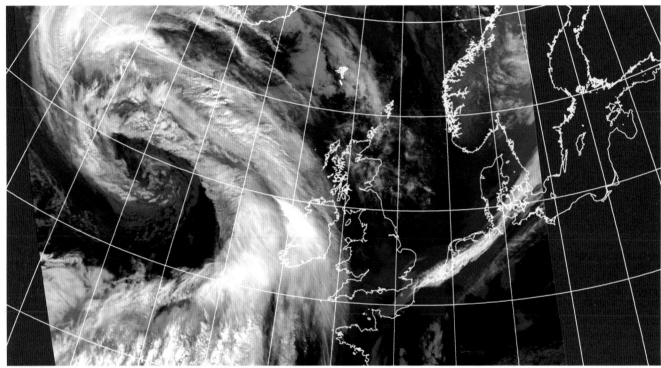

▲ **E** Satellite photo of a depression over the British Isles

Depressions form over the Atlantic Ocean. They travel from west to east across the British Isles.

All depressions follow a similar pattern. First comes the warm front. It brings a wide band of cloud and rain.

Then comes the cold front. It brings heavy showers. Eventually, the depression passes and the weather brightens up.

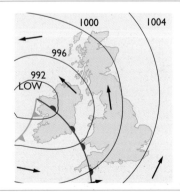

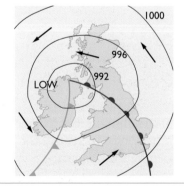

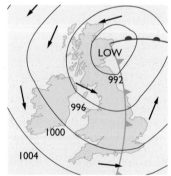

The lines on the charts are isobars. They join places with the same air pressure. Notice the direction of the winds. They blow anticlockwise around the depression.

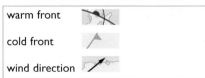

warm front

cold front

wind direction

▲ **F** Weather charts showing a depression moving across the British Isles

Weather forecasters use satellite photos, like photo E, to track depressions as they approach the British Isles. This helps them to forecast the weather on the ground. Temperature, rainfall and wind direction change as the depression moves across (cross-section G).

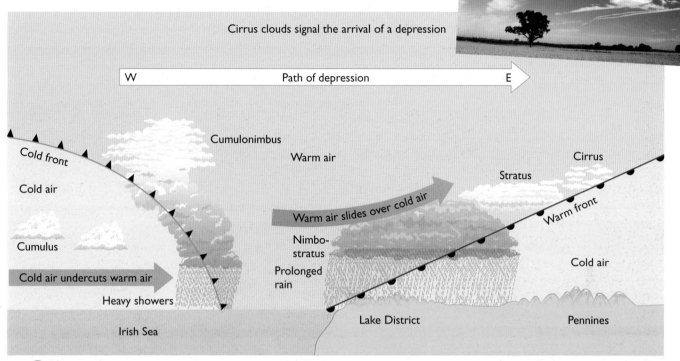

Cirrus clouds signal the arrival of a depression

W → Path of depression → E

Cold front

Cold air

Cumulus

Cold air undercuts warm air

Heavy showers

Irish Sea

Cumulonimbus

Warm air

Warm air slides over cold air

Nimbo-stratus

Prolonged rain

Lake District

Cirrus

Stratus

Warm front

Cold air

Pennines

▲ **G** Cross-section of a depression moving over the Lake District

Activities

1 Look at the charts in F. Choose the correct words to complete these sentences.
   At the centre of the depression is high/low pressure
   The depression moves from east/west to east/west across the British Isles
   First comes the warm/cold front, then comes the warm/cold front
   Winds blow clockwise/anti-clockwise around a depression

2 Study cross-section G.
   You are in the Lake District. Describe how the weather changes as a depression moves over it (study the cross-section from **right** to **left**). You should mention temperature, cloud, rainfall and wind direction (look back at F).
   Write your description in a table like this.

Weather feature	Description
Temperature	At first the air is cold. As the warm front passes ...

Assignment

A fast-moving depression is due to pass over the British Isles over the next 24 hours. The weather chart below shows the position of the depression over the Atlantic Ocean now. It is the same depression you can see in satellite photo E.

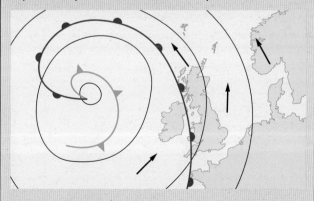

Write a weather forecast for the Lake District for the next 24 hours. You could write it like the forecast in source D on page 43. It is important that you get your forecast right. People's lives could depend on it!

2.8

What is happening to the rain in Spain?

In this case study you will find out why droughts are happening more frequently in Spain, and suggest how people can adapt to the problem.

Every year, more of us go to Spain for our holidays than anywhere else in the world. The main reason we go is for the sunny weather. Millions of British holidaymakers head for beaches along the Mediterranean coast, which, in summer, is the sunniest part of Spain (photo A).

There is a problem. All these tourists use a lot of water and, in Spain's dry climate, there isn't much to go around. What makes it worse is that Spain's climate seems to be getting hotter and drier. 2005 was the driest year in Spain since records began. There is even a suggestion that parts of Spain could turn into a desert!

▲ **A** Alicante, a Mediterranean resort

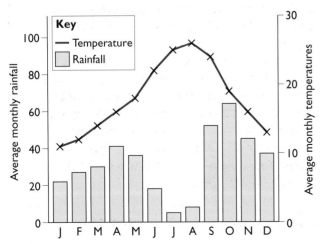

▲ **B** Climate in Alicante

Activities

I Look at graph B.

a) Write two sentences to describe the climate in Alicante. Write one sentence to describe the summer and one to describe the winter. Use these words in your sentences.

> hot   wet   dry   mild

b) When do most holidaymakers go to the Mediterranean? Why?

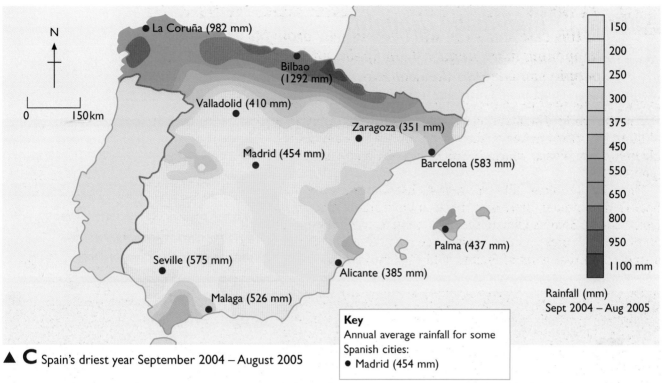

▲ **C** Spain's driest year September 2004 – August 2005

A drought is a prolonged shortage of water. What people mean by drought depends on where they live. In Britain we talk about a drought when we get a hosepipe ban after a few weeks of low rainfall! In parts of Africa a drought can last for years and cause widespread famine.

As the world gets warmer, patterns of rainfall are changing. Floods and droughts are happening more frequently.

---

2 Look at map C.
  a) What is the annual average rainfall for Alicante? Roughly, how much rain fell there in the year 2004–5?
  b) Now, look at the other cities on the map. For each city, give the annual average rainfall and say whether it was wetter or drier than normal in 2004–5.
  c) Which parts of Spain were worst affected by the drought in 2004–5?

3 Read article D.
  a) List all the effects of the drought in Spain.
  b) If you were the government minister responsible for water in Spain, what would you do to save water?

---

13 June 2005

DROUGHT IN SPAIN

Spain is suffering one of the worst droughts on record. After an unusually dry winter and spring, temperatures have begun to soar into the 30s as summer arrives. Across the country reservoirs are half empty, water is being rationed, farm crops and livestock are dying for lack of water and there is a growing risk of forest fires.

Perhaps the biggest threat is to the tourist industry. Spain attracts more than 50 million foreign visitors every year. Most of them arrive between June and September.

Eastern Spain is worst affected by the drought. Especially hard-hit are the tourist centres around the Costa Brava (near Barcelona) and the Costa Blanca (near Alicante). Swimming pools remain empty, golf clubs have been told not to use sprinklers and fountains are dry. Tourism is Spain's biggest money earner. The worry is that tourists will be put off by reports of water shortages.

▲ **D** News report of Spanish drought in 2005

Natural or man-made drought?

Apart from the north coast, where rainfall is high, Spain has a fairly dry climate. Many of the driest areas are to the east, close to the Mediterranean coast (map C on page 47). Like the rest of southern Europe and northern Africa, this region has a Mediterranean climate. Summers are hot and dry while winters are mild and wet.

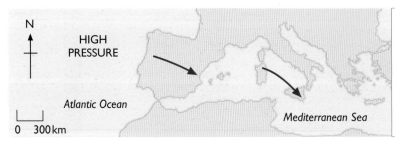

Summer

In summer the Sun is high in the sky, giving more heat.

There is high pressure over the Atlantic Ocean.

Air is pushing down so there are few clouds.

Winds bring warm dry air over the land.

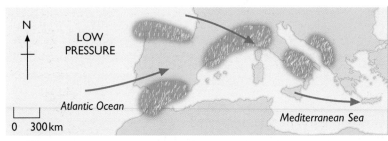

Winter

In winter the Sun is lower in the sky, giving less heat.

There is low pressure over the Atlantic Ocean.

Air is rising so more clouds form.

Winds bring moist air that produces rain.

▲ **E** The Mediterranean climate

▲ **F** A Spanish reservoir during the 2005 drought

Spain is used to summer drought. It is a normal part of a Mediterranean climate. But, when the rain does not come in winter the problem is much more serious. In 2005 reservoirs in some parts of Spain were virtually empty because they had received so little winter rain. No one is sure if this is part of a natural cycle that happens every few years, or whether Spain really is getting drier.

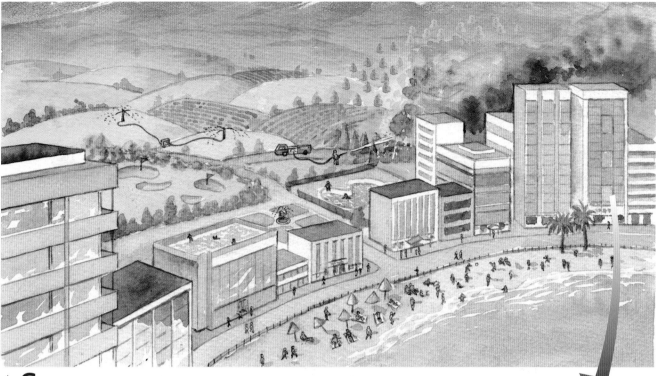

▲ **G** Water is a vital resource near the Mediterranean

The Mediterranean coast is one of the most crowded parts of Spain. As well as cities like Barcelona, Valencia and Alicante, it also attracts millions of tourists every year. New hotels and villas are still being built, many of them for British people moving to Spain. Between them, all these people use a lot of water, most of it from reservoirs.

Farming is another activity that uses water. Spain exports crops like oranges, grapes, tomatoes and lettuce to other parts of Europe. They are grown on the flat coastal land around the Mediterranean. Through the long, dry summers crops need regular irrigation to help them grow. Farmers pump the water up from wells. As a result, groundwater is being used up faster than it is replaced naturally by rainfall.

Activities

I Study source E.
Complete a large table, like this, to compare summer and winter in a Mediterranean climate.

	Summer	Winter
Sun's position		
Pressure		
Cloud		
Wind direction		
Rainfall		

2 Look carefully at drawing G.

a) Suggest how each of these people are using water. The drawing gives you clues, but you might think of more ideas for yourself.
  – a tourist   – a farmer   – a firefighter
  – a permanent resident

b) The Spanish government wants people to reduce the amount of water that they use. What arguments might each person use against having to cut their water use?
  For example, a farmer could say, 'My crops will die and I could go out of business. Export crops earn money for Spain.'

3 Do you think that drought in Spain is natural, man-made, or both? Give reasons for your answer.

Plants adapt, but how about us?

Plants that grow in a Mediterranean climate are adapted to live in hot, dry summers and mild, wet winters. They have learnt to store water and reduce moisture loss during the summer drought. Mostly, they grow, and produce their fruit, in winter and spring when more water is available. Some Mediterranean plants, like olives, grapes and oranges, have been cultivated for thousands of years.

Olive trees are evergreen. They grow slowly through the year – even in winter.

Small, waxy leaves help to reduce moisture loss in the heat.

Thick trunks can store water through the summer drought.

Trees produce their fruit in winter when more water is available.

Olives have a thick skin, also to reduce moisture loss.

Long roots help the tree to search for water in the soil.

▲ **H** An olive grove in Spain. Olive trees are adapted to the Mediterranean climate.

Activities

I Look at photo H.
  a) Draw a large sketch of an olive tree, like this.

  b) Label your sketch to show how an olive tree is adapted to the Mediterranean climate.

2 Think of ways in which people can adapt to live in a Mediterranean climate. Think of at least four. You can get some of your ideas from the way an olive tree adapts!

  For example, *People could build more reservoirs to store water in winter. The water can be used through the drought in summer.*

One third of the world's land area is desert or semi-desert. Nearly one billion people live here, including some of the world's poorest people. Many areas of semi-desert are turning into desert as a result of changing climate and people's misuse, or overuse, of the land. This process is called desertification.

Map J shows the world's deserts and the areas threatened by desertification. One of these areas is eastern Spain (photo I). Here land is turning to desert as the climate warms, water sources are used up and forest fires burn the natural vegetation.

▲ I Is this the Sahara? No, it's in Spain!

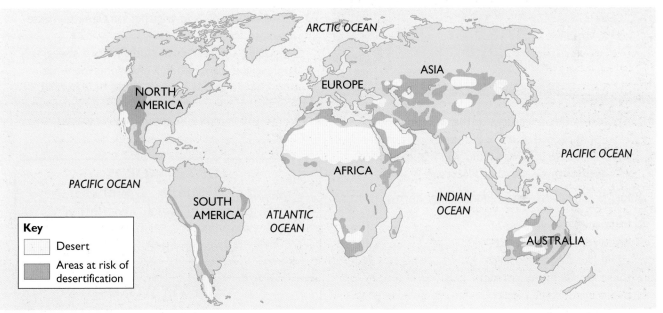

▲ J The world's deserts and areas at risk from desertification

3 Look at map J.
  a) Name at least six areas of the world where there is a risk of desertification. Which of these areas are rich, and which are poor?
  b) Spain is a rich country. How could this help it adapt to desertification? Why might the problem be greater in a poorer country?

Assignment

Tourism in Spain is threatened by drought and desertification. At the same time, climate in the UK is likely to become more like the Mediterranean is today.
Either
Advertise a holiday in Spain in the year 2050. Think about how the climate in Spain could have changed. How will holidays in Spain need to adapt to the change in climate?
Or
Advertise a seaside holiday in the UK in the year 2050. Think about how the climate in the UK could have changed. How will holidays in the UK need to adapt to the change in climate?

TEST YOURSELF

1 What is weather?

2 Look at this weather map. Describe the weather in your part of the UK. Mention at least two things.

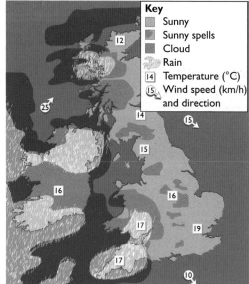

Key
- Sunny
- Sunny spells
- Cloud
- Rain
- 14 Temperature (°C)
- 15 Wind speed (km/h) and direction

3 a) Name three features of the weather you could record at a weather station.

b) What instruments would you use to record each of these weather features?

4 Name four factors that affect microclimate.

5 Make a simple version of the water cycle. Draw a circle like this and insert these words in the correct order around the circle: precipitation, evaporation, surface flow, condensation.

6 Draw a simple diagram to show convectional rain happening. You can use these labels on your diagram:
- heat from the Sun warms the ground
- air above the ground rises and cools
- water vapour condenses to form clouds. It rains

7 a) Why is it colder in the north than in the south of Britain?

b) Why is it wetter in the west than in the east of Britain?

8 Which is the odd one out in these groups of words? In each case, explain why.
a) temperature   climate   wind speed   rainfall
b) evaporation   condensation   precipitation   cloud
c) weather   wind direction   latitude   altitude
d) rain shadow   front   convection   relief

NOW, FOR A CHALLENGE!

9 What is the difference between weather and climate?

Illustrate your answer, referring to the weather and climate in a named area you have studied.

10 How can changes in weather or climate create a hazard for people?

Using a named case study, write a paragraph to describe how, either, a change in the weather, or a change in the climate, could be a hazard.

These are the words you should try to learn for this unit:

TOP TEN WORDS
weather   climate   temperature
precipitation   wind   water cycle
evaporation   condensation
microclimate   cloud

MORE KEY WORDS
weather station   rain gauge
thermometer   barometer
water store   water vapour
surface flow   groundwater flow
convectional rain   relief rain
frontal rain   front   rain shadow   aspect

IMPRESS YOUR TEACHER!
meteorologist   meteorological Office
air pressure   depression   isobar
warm front   cold front   drought
temperate climate
mediterranean climate   irrigation
desertification

UNIT 3

Settlement

▲ Times Square in New York

New York is a city in the USA. It is a very large
settlement. Settlements are places where people live.
Over half the people in the world now live in cities.

- Would you like to live here? Why, or why not?
- What do you think are the best things about cities?
- What are the worst things?
- Why do so many people live in cities?

3.1   Who needs neighbours?

You probably live in an urban area – a built-up area which is part of a town or city. This is not just a guess! Nine out of every ten people in Britain live in a town or city.

Two hundred years ago the situation was quite different. At that time most people lived in villages in rural areas.

People usually move to cities to find jobs and for a better quality of life. However, some cities have high levels of unemployment, crime and pollution.

▲ **A** *Emmerdale*, set in the Yorkshire Dales, a rural area

▲ **B** *EastEnders*, set in London, an urban area

Activities

1 Look at the two photos. They are from two well-known TV soaps: *Emmerdale* and *EastEnders*.
   What would you like or dislike about living in each of these places?

2 Read the list of features in the box below. Are they features of urban or rural areas? Sort them into two lists, one to describe each type of area.

> tall buildings   fields
> trees   shopping centres
> traffic jams   concrete
> parks   pollution   villages
> housing estates   farms
> factories   litter   fresh air
> isolated buildings
> few people   open space
> narrow lanes
> entertainment
> many people

▲ **C** *Neighbours*, set in the suburbs of Melbourne

Neighbours is another popular TV soap set in the city of Melbourne, Australia. Because it is near the edge of the city, the area is neither really urban nor really rural. This type of place is called a suburb. Many people have moved out from city centres to live in suburban areas. This has happened in Britain as well as in Australia.
Some villages in rural areas, close to cities, are also growing to be more like suburbs. The difference between urban and rural is getting smaller.

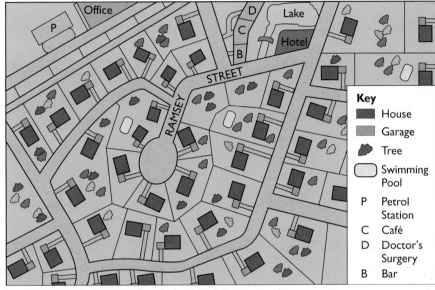

▲ **D** The area of Melbourne where *Neighbours* is set

Key
■	House
■	Garage
🌳	Tree
◯	Swimming Pool
P	Petrol Station
C	Café
D	Doctor's Surgery
B	Bar

3 Study the information on this page.
 a) List the features of a suburban area.
 b) What are the advantages of living in an area like this? Can you think of any disadvantages?

4 Write your own scene for an episode of a soap. Include information in your story describing life in this type of area. You can choose characters from the soap or make up your own characters.

Homework

5 Watch an episode of a TV soap.
 a) Look for any other features of an urban, suburban or rural area. Add these features to your list.
 b) Think about the area where you live. Which type of area is it most like? What do you like or dislike about living there?

▲ **E** Janae and Boyd Hoyland from *Neighbours*

3.2 Settlement sites

The place where a settlement is built is its site. Most settlements in Britain date back over a thousand years to the times of the Celts, Romans, Saxons and Vikings. The sites they chose depended on a number of natural advantages, including the shape of the land, the climate and what resources were available. The settlements that grew were those that had the most advantages.

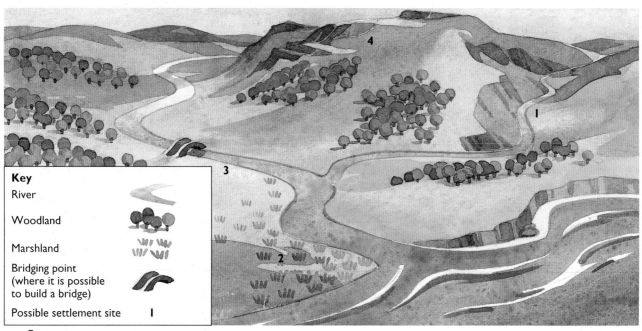

Key

River

Woodland

Marshland

Bridging point (where it is possible to build a bridge)

Possible settlement site   1

▲ **A** An area of Britain before any settlements were built

Activities

1 Look at drawing A. It shows four possible sites for a settlement in an area of Britain.

2 Read the list of natural advantages in the table on the right. These are what early settlers looked for when choosing a site.

a) On a copy of the table, tick the boxes for the natural advantages which each site has.

b) Which is the best site for a settlement? Give reasons.

c) Which site might be preferred by people who were:

i)   farmers

ii) local warriors?

Natural advantage Site	1	2	3	4
Water supply – close to river for drinking water				
Defence – hilltop sites have good views and are easy to defend				
Building material – close to woodland or rocky hillside				
Farmland – flat land usually has good soil for growing crops				
Fuel – wood needed to burn for warmth and cooking				
Flood prevention – sites away from rivers and marshland are safer				
Rivers – provide transport but must be narrow enough to bridge				
Shelter – close to steep slopes or woodland				

... and shapes

If you look at a map, you will notice that all settlements have different shapes.

In lowland parts of Britain it is common to find nucleated settlements, where buildings are grouped together. Settlements with this shape often grew around a road junction or river crossing. Sometimes a wall was built around the settlement for protection. In upland areas it is more common to find dispersed settlements, where buildings are spread further apart. Here people needed more land to grow their crops or graze animals. Linear settlements are long and thin. They are more likely to be found along a narrow valley or close to a road or river.

▲ **B** Warkworth, Northumberland

3 Look at photos B, C and D. They show settlements with different shapes.
  a) Match each photo with one of the three shapes – nucleated, dispersed or linear.
  b) Write a sentence to describe the shape of the settlement in each photo.

4 The map below shows the area in drawing A. Choose the most likely site for each of the three types of settlement.
  a) On a large copy of the map, draw each of the settlements at the sites you have chosen. Make each one the correct shape. Add roads to the map to link the settlements. Think about the best route for each road.
  b) Which settlement on your map would be most likely to grow? Explain why.

Homework

5 Find out more about the settlement that you live in. Is it a village, a town or part of a large city? What site was the settlement built on? Why was that site chosen? What shape is the settlement? When did people start living there? How has it grown?

▲ **C** Isle of Skye, Scotland

▶ **D** Ironbridge, Shropshire

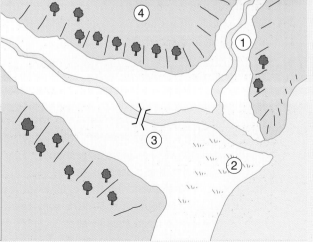

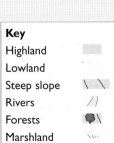

Key

Highland	
Lowland	
Steep slope	\ \
Rivers	//
Forests	🌳\
Marshland	\ۭ\

3.3 Settlements and their functions

Settlements can vary in size from the smallest hamlet, with just a few homes, to the largest city with millions of people. The larger the settlement, the more shops and services it has. You can arrange settlements in order of their size and importance. This is called a settlement hierarchy (diagram A).

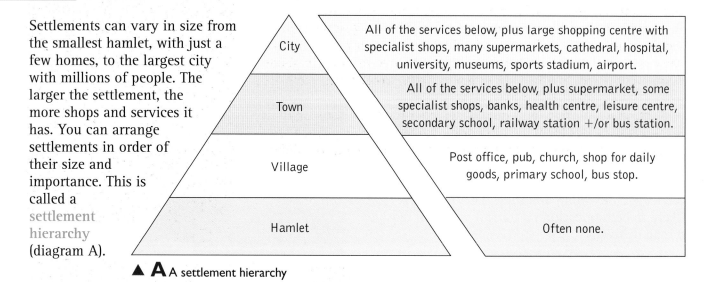

City	All of the services below, plus large shopping centre with specialist shops, many supermarkets, cathedral, hospital, university, museums, sports stadium, airport.
Town	All of the services below, plus supermarket, some specialist shops, banks, health centre, leisure centre, secondary school, railway station +/or bus station.
Village	Post office, pub, church, shop for daily goods, primary school, bus stop.
Hamlet	Often none.

▲ **A** A settlement hierarchy

Activities

1 Look at map B. It shows settlements in East Yorkshire. Draw a table like the one below to compare villages, towns and cities on the map.

Type of settlement	How many on map?	Example	Distance apart	Population range	Likely shops & services
Village		South Cave			

To complete your table:
a) Count the number of settlements of each size on map B. Write the number in column 2.
b) Choose one example of a settlement of each size. Write the name in column 3.
c) Measure the distance to the nearest settlement of the same size. Write this information in column 4.
d) Find the range of population from the key. Write this in column 5.
e) List the likely shops and services in column 6. You can find the information in diagram A.

2 Read the list of statements below. Which are true and which are false? Write a list of the true statements, entitled 'Rules about settlements'.
• There are more large settlements than small ones.
• There are more small settlements than large ones.
• Smaller settlements are closer together.
• Larger settlements are closer together.
• The larger the settlement the more services it provides.
• The smaller the settlement the more services it provides.
• More people live in large settlements.
• More people live in small settlements.

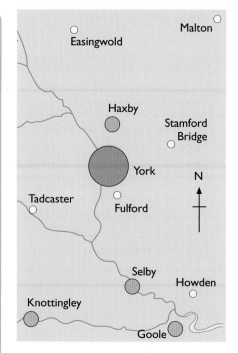

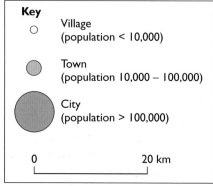

Key
○ Village (population < 10,000)
◓ Town (population 10,000 – 100,000)
⬤ City (population > 100,000)

0 ———— 20 km

▲ **B** Settlements in East Yorkshire

The original function of each settlement depended on its location.

Some early settlements grew as defensive towns, to protect their inhabitants against attacks from enemies. Others grew as market towns, where farmers and people from neighbouring settlements would come to buy and sell goods. Settlements built near rivers or the coast were often ports, where ships were able to bring in goods from other places and take other goods away. Other settlements grew as industrial towns or holiday resorts.

Settlements change over time. The modern function of many settlements differs from its original function. For example, many villages that were once fishing ports have now turned into holiday resorts.

▲ **C** Hull

▲ **D** Beverley

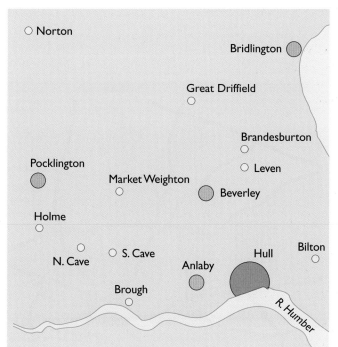

▲ **E** Bridlington

---

3 Look at photos C, D and E.
  a) Identify the function of each of the settlements.
  b) Locate each settlement on map B. Write a sentence to describe the location of each settlement.
  c) In each case, explain why its location is well suited to its function.

Homework

4 Find out the original function of your own settlement. Has its function changed? If so, how? What are its functions now?

Draw a shield for your settlement, decorated with symbols to illustrate its functions today.

3.4   Shops and services

As you know, the larger the settlement the more shops and services it has. Large towns and cities often have more than one shopping centre. Where people choose to shop depends on what they want to buy. These days some people also do their shopping on the Internet.

Things that we buy often, like bread and newspapers, are convenience goods. We buy them at the most convenient place. Things that we buy less often, like clothes or furniture, are comparison goods. We like to shop around and compare them before we buy.

▲ **A** Shopping goods

▲ **B** A high street shopping centre

▲ **C** An out-of-town shopping centre

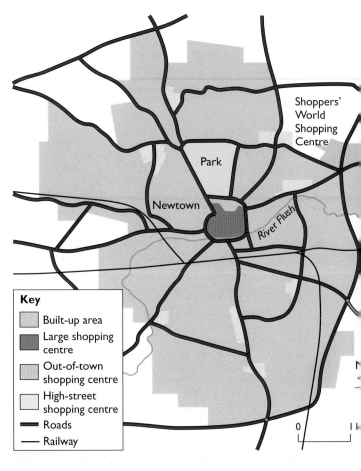

Key

- Built-up area
- Large shopping centre
- Out-of-town shopping centre
- High-street shopping centre
- Roads
- Railway

▲ **D** Shopping centres in a city

Activities

1 Look at the goods in drawing A.
Sort them into two groups – convenience and comparison goods.

2 Look at photos B and C.
   a) Where would you buy the goods in drawing A? Write three shopping lists – one for each shopping centre and one for the internet.
   b) Choose one item from each list. Explain why you would buy it at that shopping centre, or on the internet.
   c) Where would you prefer to shop? Why?

3 Suggest two reasons why the Government might not want any more new out-of-town shopping centres to be built.

Shopping Survey

1 **How often do you shop here?**
Every day
Once a week, or more 4
Once a month, or more 12
Less than once a month 56
.... 28

2 **How far do you travel to come here?**
Less than 1 km
Between 1 and 2 km 9
Between 2 and 5 km 24
More than 5 km 47
.... 20

3 **How do you travel here?**
On foot
By car 3
By train or bus 62
Other 26
.... 9

4 **What is the main thing you come here to buy?**
Food
Clothes or shoes 8
Large household goods 54
Other 17
.... 21

▶ **E** Results of a shopping survey carried out at a large out-of-town shopping centre

Local investigation

How do the shopping habits of people who use a local high street shopping centre compare with those who use a large out-of-town centre?

Work in a group. Do a shopping survey at your local shopping centre. You can use a copy of the shopping survey sheet above, or make up your own. Work with a partner.

Each pair will need: a copy of the survey sheet, a clipboard and a pencil.

At the shopping centre:
• Interview shoppers. Decide how many shoppers each pair in the group will interview (try to do 100 between the whole group). Include as many types of people as you can, to represent all the shoppers at the centre.
• Mark the correct box beside the answer each shopper gives. Keep a tally of the answers you get.

In the classroom:
• Share all the answers with the other members of your group. Count the total number of marks for each answer.
• Think of ways to display the results using suitable graphs or diagrams and draw these.
  You could record your results on a database, using a computer and a graph-drawing package to draw your graphs.
• Describe the graphs and diagrams that you have drawn and explain what they show.
• Compare the results of the survey at your local shopping centre with a large shopping centre. You can use the results shown in E. Write four paragraphs to compare:
  – How often people shop there
  – How they travel there
  – How far they travel to get there
  – What they buy there.

3.5   Patterns in cities

You will find the oldest part of most cities at the centre. This is where the original settlement was built. Over the years, cities grow outwards as new buildings are built around the edges. This was how Bristol grew, for example (A).

In any city, as you travel out in a line – or transect – from the city centre, you will notice a similar pattern (B).

At the centre of a city is the central business district (CBD), where most shops and offices are. There are also theatres, hotels, restaurants and museums. Many old buildings have been replaced with modern office blocks or high-rise apartments because land is expensive.

Around the CBD is the inner city. It used to be an area with rows of old terraced housing and large factories. In recent years the area may have been redeveloped – the houses improved, or replaced with new homes, and the factories demolished.

Beyond the inner city are the inner suburbs. They grew through the twentieth century as transport improved and people began to live further from the city centre. Many of the houses are semi-detached, with their own gardens.

Further out, close to the edge of the city, are the outer suburbs. The houses are modern, many are detached with gardens and garages. There are also new industrial estates and out-of-town shopping centres, built here because land is cheaper.

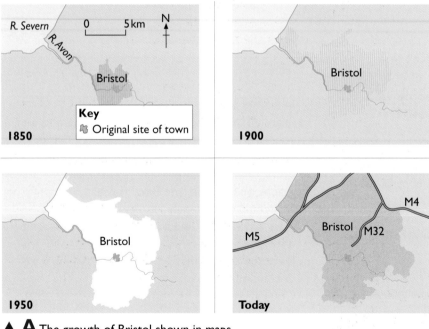

▲ **A** The growth of Bristol shown in maps

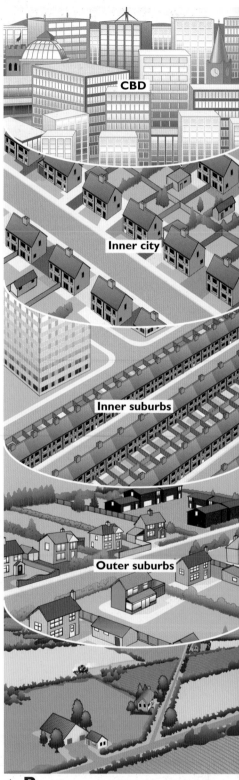

▲ **B** Transect of a city

▲ C

▲ D

▲ E

▲ F

Activities

1 Look at the maps in A.
   a) Where was the original site of Bristol?
   b) How had the city changed by 1850?
   c) Describe the way that Bristol has grown since 1850. Mention how the shape of the city changed.

2 Look at transect B.
   a) Match each area on the transect with one of the photos – C, D, E and F.
   b) In each case describe the area with the help of the photos. Here are features that you could mention.

terraced houses	shops	garages
no gardens	high-rise blocks	no garages
detached houses	on-street parking	
semi-detached houses	heavy traffic	gardens

3 a) In which area of the city would you be most likely to:
   • go to the cinema?
   • get your bike stolen?
   • go to a good school?
   • suffer from asthma?
   • build an extension?
   • see cars parked on the road?
   b) In each case, give a reason.

Homework

4 Think about your nearest city.
   a) Draw a transect, like this, from the city centre to the edge of the city.

   city centre | inner city | inner suburb | outer suburb

   b) Name one place in your city to match each of the areas on the transect.
   c) Produce an advert for a home in one area of the city. You could get ideas by looking at some real adverts.

3.6

Why did London grow?

In this case study you will look at historical evidence of London's growth to compare past and present.

I was in the Roman army of the Emperor Claudius, which conquered Britain in AD43. We landed near Dover and then marched north, seizing control from the local tribes. The main obstacle was the River Thames which, towards the sea, was too wide to cross, and its banks too marshy to build a bridge. Eventually we found a place to build a bridge as close to the sea as possible. But the Britons attacked and we had to defend the bridge. Soldiers built a camp around the bridge. Soon there were other people living there and it grew into a city. We called it Londinium. The city became the main port in Britain with boats coming to and from Rome. It was also the centre of our road network, linking all the cities we built. Within 50 years, Londinium was the capital city of Britain.

▲ **A** Roman London

Activities

1 Look at the drawing of Roman London (Londinium) and read what the soldier says.
   a) List all the features that led to the development of this settlement.
   b) London was the lowest bridging point on the River Thames. Explain what you think this means.

2 Draw a sketch map to show the main features of the drawing. Label the features that show the advantages of this site for a settlement.

3 Write a letter from the commander of the Roman army in Britain to the Emperor Claudius, asking him for money and more soldiers to build a city. Persuade the Emperor that this is a good place for a capital city.

▲ **B** Covent Garden Market originally opened in 1670. It sold fruit and vegetables for the growing population of London. Eventually it became too congested and in 1970 a new market was built further from the centre. Covent Garden now sells clothes and souvenirs.

▲ **C** The Tower of London was built by William the Conqueror in 1066. It was built to defend London from invaders, but is now a tourist attraction. In the background is the City of London where many large banks and other companies have their headquarters.

◄ **D** Waterloo Station was built in 1848. All the main railway stations were built during the nineteenth century. This marked the start of London's most rapid period of growth. Eurostar trains now go to Paris and Brussels from London.

▲ **E** The London Dock was built in 1805. It was the first of many docks built on the River Thames, downstream from London. Many of London's factories were built close to the docks. By 1980 all the docks had closed.

4 Study all the information on these two pages.
  a) Draw a table like the one below, listing all the functions that London has had.
  b) Give evidence for each of these functions.
  c) State whether or not it still has each function. One has been started for you.

Function	Evidence	Does it still have this function?
Port	the docks	

5 If a Roman soldier were to return to London today he might be amazed to see how it has grown.

When we built a bridge I never imagined that it would end up like this!

Work with a partner to role-play the conversation between the Roman soldier and someone who lives in London today.

If you are the soldier, think of the questions he might ask.

If you are the Londoner, try to answer the soldier's questions from the information on this page.

How has London changed?

Improvements in transport during the nineteenth and twentieth centuries helped London to grow. In 1800 places like Hampstead were villages well outside the built-up area of London. Today, Hampstead is a suburb quite close to central London – only ten minutes away on the Underground. London is now a conurbation – a very large urban area into which many separate settlements have merged.

▲ **F** The view from Hampstead, shown in Constable's painting of 1834

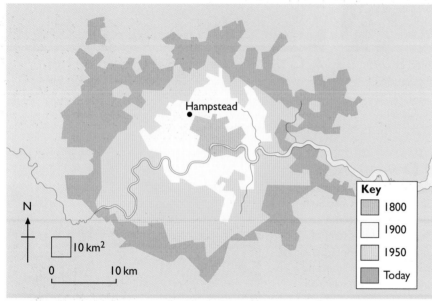

▲ **G** London's growth since 1800

1800	1,000,000
1850	3,000,000
1900	6,500,000
1950	8,000,000
2000	7,000,000

▲ **H** Population change in London

▲ **I** The view from Hampstead today

Activities

1 Look at map G, which shows the growth of London since 1800.
  a) Estimate the area of London at each of the four dates shown on the key. To do this accurately, draw a grid on tracing paper using the 10 km² shown on the scale. Place it over the map. Count the number of squares which London covered at each date.
  b) Draw a bar graph to show London's growth. Use a grid like the top one here.
2 Look at table H, which shows the change of population in London since 1800. Draw a line graph to show London's population change. Use a grid like the bottom one here.

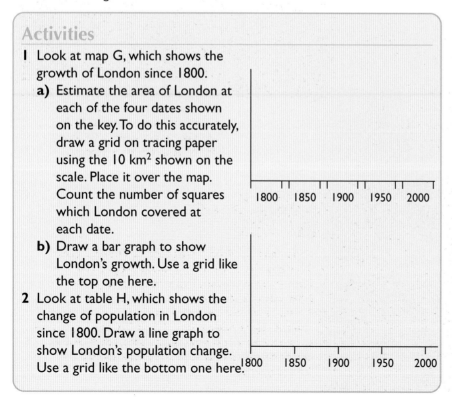

Assignment

Write an extract for a history book about the growth of London.

Compare London as it was at the beginning of the nineteenth century with London today. Use all the information from this investigation. Include each of these words in your extract:

urban   village   railway
conurbation   suburb
rural

3.7 What services can you find?

In this case study you will use a map and photos to compare services in settlements of different sizes.

You have learnt that the larger that a settlement the more shops and services it will have. Now, you are going to investigate whether this is true for the city of York (map D on page 68) and the settlements around it (photos A, B and C). Then, you will plan a further investigation to find out what difference a new out-of-town shopping centre will make to York and its neighbouring settlements.

Activities

1 Look at the photos on this page. They show some settlements near York. What types of shops and services can you see in each photo?

2 Find each settlement on the 1:50,000 OS map extract on the next page. Give the four-figure grid reference for each settlement.

3 Study the key to the services on the 1:50,000 OS map, below.

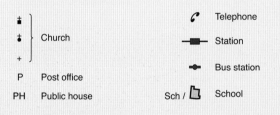

☧ ☩ +	Church	✆	Telephone
		▬■	Station
		●■	Bus station
P	Post office		
PH	Public house	Sch / ⬠	School

a) Name the services that can be found at these six-figure references. Which settlement are they in?
677 552   668 525   630 512   600 517

b) How many types of services can you find in York? Give a six-figure grid reference for one example of each type of service you can find.

▼ **A** Warthill

Services: church, pub, phone, primary school

▼ **B** Dunnington

Shops and services: 2 churches, 2 pubs, phone, 2 supermarkets, post office, newsagent, butcher, chemist, florist, hair salon, estate agent, off-licence, doctor, dentist, primary school

◀ **C** Haxby

Shops and services: 5 estate agents, 4 banks, 3 pubs, 3 supermarkets, 3 chemists, 3 clothes shops, 2 churches, 2 take-away restaurants, 2 stationers, 2 greengrocers, 2 hair salons, 2 vets, 2 newsagents, 2 butchers, 2 restaurants, post office, optician, dry cleaner, off-licence, insurance agent, baker, electrical shop, DIY shop, travel agent, picture framer, carpet shop, antique shop, health centre, doctor, dentist, ambulance station, garage, solicitor, 2 primary schools

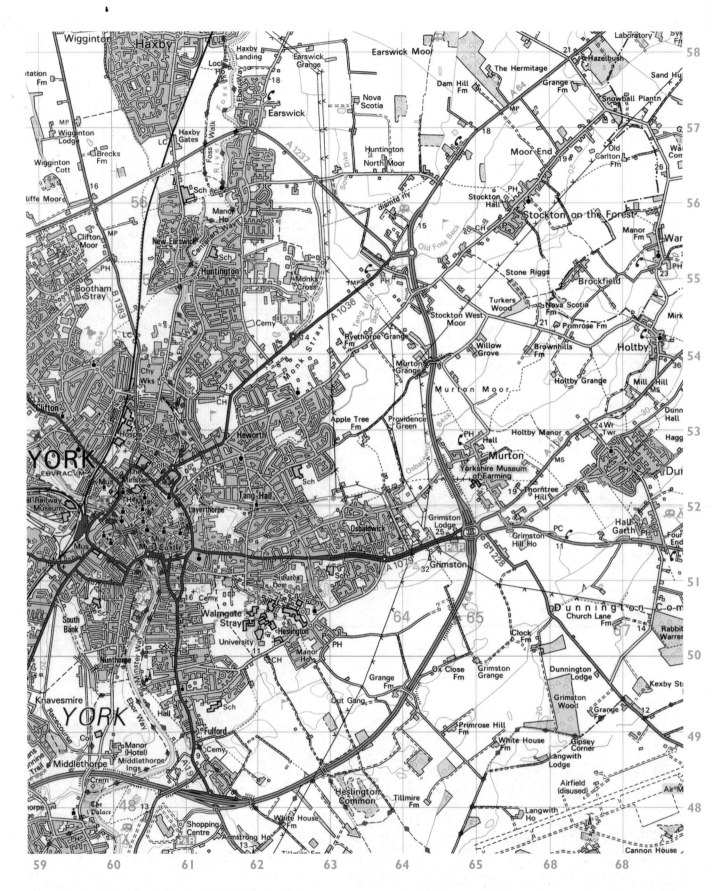

▲ **D** York. Reproduced from the 2006 1:50,000 Ordnance Survey map of York by permission of the Controller of HMSO © Crown Copyright.

What difference does size make?

Activities

1 Look at table E. It shows the population of four of the settlements on the map.

Settlement	Population
Dunnington	3,000
Haxby	9,400
Warthill	250
York	104,000

E

a) Rank the settlements in order of population.
b) Draw a bar chart of population with the bars in that order.

2 a) From the map, estimate the size of each settlement. (Each square on the map is 1 km².)
b) Rank the settlements in order of their size. Draw a bar chart of settlement size with the bars in that order.
c) Compare the two bar charts. Explain the link between the population and the size of settlements.

3 a) Count the total number of shops and services found in Warthill, Dunnington and Haxby (listed on page 67). Rank the three settlements in order of the number of shops and services.

▲ F York city centre

b) Draw a bar chart of the number of shops and services with the bars in that order.
c) Compare all the bar charts. Explain the link between the number of shops and services a settlement has and its size.
d) What shops and services would you expect to find in York and cannot find in the smaller settlements?

▲ G Monk's Cross shopping centre outside York

Assignment

A new out-of-town shopping centre has opened to the north of York at Monk's Cross (62 54).

a) Suggest how this might affect the shops and services in the four settlements you have looked at on the map, and what differences this may make to the shopping habits of people living there.
b) Plan an investigation in the area on the map, to find out whether or not your ideas are correct.

3.8 How will the 2012 Olympics change London?

In this case study you will examine the plans for the 2012 Olympics and think about what difference they will make to one of the poorest parts of London.

In July 2005, London won the bid to host the Olympic and Paralympic Games in 2012. The Games will be held at venues all around London (map B), but the main venue will be the new Olympic Park in the Lower Lea Valley in East London (pages 72 and 73). One of the reasons that London's bid was successful was its plan to regenerate the Lower Lea Valley as a result of the Olympics. It is in one of London's most deprived areas.

Urban regeneration is often an important part of plans for sporting events. The 2002 Commonwealth Games in Manchester helped to regenerate the city. It created new jobs, improved the environment and led to better living standards in the city. The hope is that the 2012 Olympics will do the same for London.

▲ **A** Celebrations in Trafalgar Square when London won the 2012 Olypmic bid

Activities

1 Look at map A, or use an interactive version of the map.

To find an interactive map go to the London 2012 website at www.london2012.org/en/ and click on *Our vision*, then on *Interactive map*.

a) Draw a large table like the one below.

b) List all the Olympic venues in London in column 1. Start with the Olympic Park.

c) List the sports that will be held at each venue in Column 2. Use the key to help you.

2 a) Describe the location of the Olympic Park on map B.

b) Explain why this location was chosen.

3 a) Do you think that London was the best city in the UK to choose for holding the Olympics? Give reasons for your answer.

b) Think of reasons for choosing your city (or your nearest city) to hold the Olympics.

Key

Athletics	Boxing	Fencing	Martial arts	Tennis	Weightlifting
Archery	Canoeing	Football	5* Pentathlon	3* Triathlon	Water polo
Badminton	Cycling	Gymnastics	Swimming	Volleyball	Wrestling
Basketball	Diving	Hockey	Shooting		
Beach volleyball	Equestrian	Handball	Table tennis		

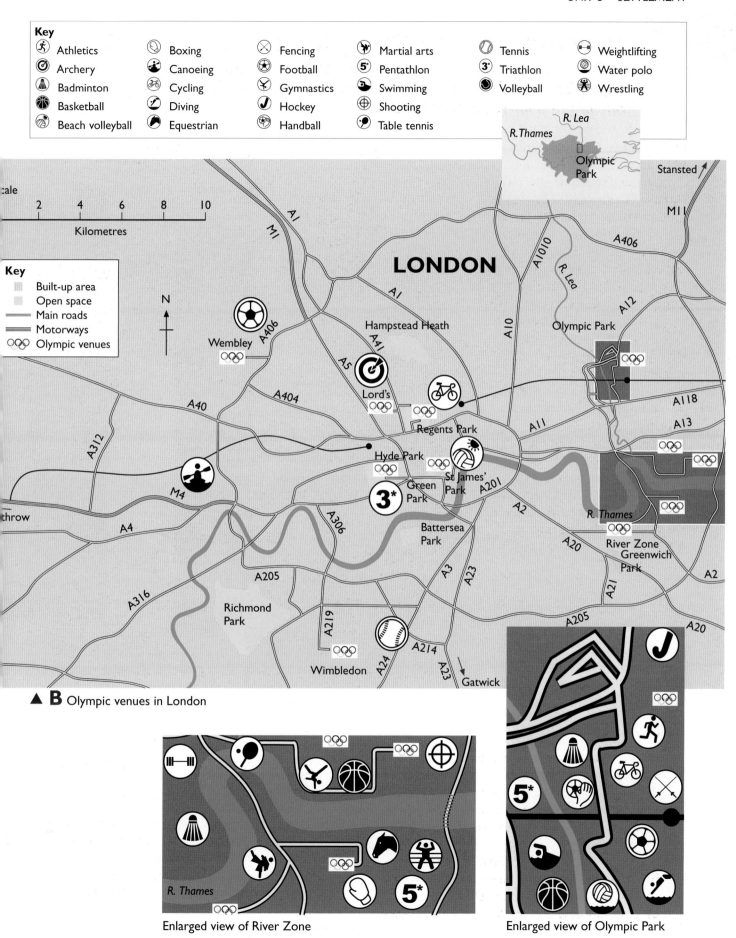

Key
- Built-up area
- Open space
- Main roads
- Motorways
- Olympic venues

▲ **B** Olympic venues in London

Enlarged view of River Zone

Enlarged view of Olympic Park

How will the Lea Valley change?

The Lower Lea Valley was once a thriving industrial area to the east of London. In the past it has been home to brickyards, gas works, flour mills and power stations. Today, most of the old industries have closed down, leaving behind a wasteland of derelict buildings and polluted ground (photo D).

Plans to regenerate the area have been around for a long time. The Olympic Games could be the ideal opportunity to make this happen.

▲ **C** Aerial view of the site of the Olympic Park

The Olympic site
200 hectares of mainly wasteland with some factories.
- It includes the River Lea, canals and other small waterways.
- It is surrounded by major roads that link with the national motorway network.
- It is beside Stratford International Railway Station, on the Channel Tunnel Rail Link between London and Europe.
- Polluted soil will need to be cleaned before building starts.
- More than 13 km of overhead power lines will need to be moved underground.

▲ **D** What the Lea Valley looks like now

The Olympic Park

- An 80,000-seater stadium will host the opening and closing ceremonies, as well as athletics events.
- There will be an Aquatic Centre (swimming), a Hockey Centre, Velodrome (cycling), and other indoor arenas.
- All the venues will be within walking distance of each other and from the Olympic Village.
- The Olympic Village will contain accommodation for every athlete (17,000 beds).
- 240,000 people per hour are expected to arrive at the Olympic Park by tube, train or bus

Activities

1 Look at photo C. Draw a simple sketch map like this to show the site of the Olympic Stadium. Label –
River Lea
A11
Stratford
    International
    Station
Mainline railway to
    London
Olympic Park
Olympic Stadium site

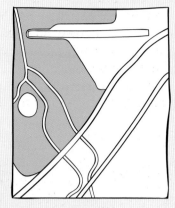

2 Identify the advantages and disadvantages of the Olympic site. Write them in a table, like this. One is done for you.

Advantages	Disadvantages
Most of the land is unused. It is wasteland.	

3 You are going to compare the Lea Valley now with what it will look like when the Olympic Park is complete.
   a) Go to the London 2012 website at www.london2012.org/en/
   b) Under *London 2012 images* click on *View picture gallery*.
   c) Under *Image library* choose *View images to download*.
   d) Next, under *Venue and site computer-generated images*, click *View gallery*.
   e) You will see a large number of images of Olympic venues. Choose three images you like of the Olympic Park (be sure they are of the Olympic Park).
   f) Print the images to stick into your book.
   g) Compare the Lea Valley now with what it will look like when the Olympic Park is complete. Describe all the changes you see.

Homework

4 Draw a plan for your own Olympic Park, including all the features listed in the box.

What will the Olympics do for us?

The Lower Lea Valley forms the boundary between the boroughs of Newham, Hackney, Tower Hamlets and Waltham Forest (map F). They include some of the most deprived communities in London.

Unemployment in the area is high and so are other signs of deprivation. By providing new employment opportunities, it is hoped that the Olympics will bring new prosperity to the area.

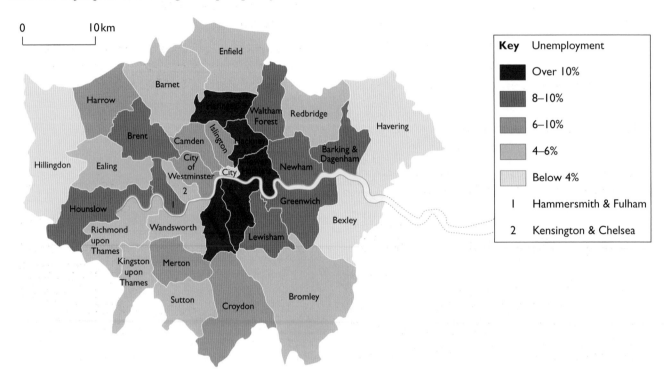

▲ E Unemployment rates in London

Average income
Newham £27,600
London £34,600

Unemployment
Newham 9.4%
London 7.0%

Life expectancy for men
Newham 73.7
London 76.0

Violent crime
Newham 32.8 per 1,000
London 25.2 per 1,000

Educational qualifications (people with degrees)
Newham 15.5%
London 30.8%

Home ownership (households owning their home)
Newham 42.4%   London 55.5%

▲ F Newham is one of the most deprived parts of London

Benefits of the Olympics for London

- An estimated 12,000 permanent jobs in new businesses will be created in the area of the Olympic Park, as well as thousands of temporary jobs before and during the Games.

- Wasteland in the Lower Lea Valley will be cleared to create London's largest new park for over 100 years.

- There will be 9,000 new homes in and around the Olympic Park once the Games are over. Half of these will be affordable homes and will be for sale or rent.

- It will speed up improvements to London's transport system, with new rail lines through Stratford due to be completed by 2012.

- State-of-the-art sports facilities will be available for Londoners to use after the Games are over.

- Previous Olympic cities have improved their image around the world. It is hoped the Olympics will do the same for London.

... but, there are problems too

- Londoners will bear much of the cost of the Games. Their taxes will rise to pay for it.

- Remaining factories on the Olympic site will be demolished and businesses will have to move. Some jobs will be lost, forcing some people to move.

- There will be lots of noise, dust and disruption for local residents while the Olympic Park is under construction.

- House prices in East London are likely to rise. This might be good for homeowners, but not for people who want to rent or buy a house.

Activities

1 Look at map F.
 a) What is the unemployment rate in Newham?
 b) How does it compare to the rest of London?

2 How is unemployment linked to other signs of deprivation?
 Choose two other signs of deprivation in photo G. Write a sentence for each one to explain how they are linked with unemployment. For example: *Unemployment is linked with low home ownership. Without a job you cannot get a mortgage to buy a home.*

3 How could the Olympics help to reduce deprivation in Newham? Suggest at least two ways.

Assignment

Will the 2012 Olympic Games change London for the better, or for worse?
 Imagine that you are one of these people:

- a school pupil in Newham
- a homeowner in East London
- a factory worker in the Lower Lea Valley
- the director of a large hotel company
- a promising, young British athlete
- the Mayor of London.

Do you think the Olympics will change London for the better, or for the worse? Think of arguments to support your view.
 In your role, you are going to take part in a televised debate on the Olympics. Prepare a short speech to explain the reasons for your views on the Olympics.

3.9   Can we make cities more sustainable?

In this case study you will think about the size of your ecological footprint, then look at ways that people in cities could live more sustainably.

We all use resources – things like food, water and fuel that we need in our daily lives. Think about all the resources that you use in your home every day. Stop reading this page for a minute and really think ...

It's a lot, isn't it? Now, multiply the amount of resources that you use by the number of houses in your street. Then multiply again by the number of streets in your city (it's likely to be hundreds). You can see why cities use so many resources.

It doesn't stop there. Think how many cities there are in the world, and multiply once more. Cities are now using the world's resources faster than they can be replaced. This is not sustainable.

Electricity comes from power stations. Power stations burn fuel (coal, gas or oil). Burning fuel produces gases that pollute the air and contribute to global warming.

Food grows on farms. It takes about one hectare of land to feed a person, but more if you eat meat. Much of our food is grown abroad and is flown here. This uses more fuel.

Water comes from the ground or is collected in large reservoirs. Some places get too much water, while others don't get enough.

Fuels, like oil and gas, are drilled from rocks beneath the land or sea. We use them to run our cars and to heat our homes. Oil and gas are likely to run out in your lifetime.

Products, like clothes and electrical goods, are produced in factories using raw materials. Many products we use are now made abroad.

Waste is thrown in the bin. Most of it ends up being burnt, or dumped in huge landfill sites in the ground. Less than 20% of our waste is recycled.

▲ **A** A city uses resources

The street you can see in photo A does not take up much space, but, look at the resources people use. Altogether, the people on that street use up quite a lot of space!

Another way to think about this is your ecological footprint. This is the amount of space on the planet that is needed to produce all the resources you use. The more resources you use in your daily life, the greater your ecological footprint.

On the left is the footprint for an average person in the UK. If everyone in the world lived like this we would need five planets! Next to it is the footprint for for an average person living in Africa. If everyone in the world lived like this there would be more than enough space on our planet. If we are to live sustainably, then all our footprints together should be no bigger than the planet.

The average person in Africa's ecological footprint

The average person in the UK's ecological footprint

▲ **B** Europe at night

Activities

1 Look at the street in photo A.
   a) List the resources that people use. (Remember that the air and the ground are resources too.)
   b) Choose one resource as an example. Explain how using this resource affects the planet.

2 Look at photo B.
   a) What are the dots?
   b) Why are they so bright?
   c) What does the photo tell us about the amount of electricity people use in Europe?
   d) What would you expect a similar photo of Africa to show?

3 Work out the size of your ecological footprint.
   a) Go to the Earthday website at www.earthday.net. Click on *Ecological Footprint.*

   b) Answer the questions to work out your footprint. If everyone lived like you, how many planets would we need?

4 How could you reduce the size of your ecological footprint? Think of at least five things you could do.

What would a sustainable city be like?

A sustainable city would be one that did no harm to the environment and did not use up the Earth's resources faster than they can be replaced. At the moment, most cities are not like that. In fact, just the opposite – they are unsustainable.

We have got so used to our present lifestyle that it is hard to imagine what a sustainable city might be like. Fortunately, we have an example.

At Beddington, in south London, is a new community with 100 homes. It is called BedZED – Beddington Zero Energy Development. The designers claim that it is environmentally friendly and uses zero energy!

▲ **C** BedZED

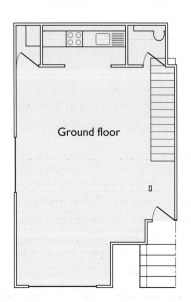

Ground floor

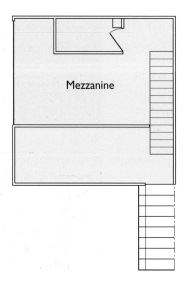

Mezzanine

◀ **D** Plan of a BedZED apartment

Apartments at BedZED are designed to provide integrated living space and workspace.

The ground floor includes living area, kitchen and toilet.

The mezzanine (first-floor gallery) includes work area, sleeping area and bathroom.

Energy

- Heat loss from buildings is reduced by good insulation of roof, walls and floor. Windows are triple glazed.
- A heat exchanger in the wind-driven ventilation system recovers heat from stale air.
- South-facing windows make maximum use of solar energy. Roofs have solar panels to convert the Sun's energy into electricity.
- Kitchens are fitted with energy-saving appliances and low-energy light bulbs in every room.

Water

- Water-efficient appliances, such as washing machines that consume less water.
- Low-volume baths and dual-flush toilets also use less water.
- Rainwater is collected from roofs and stored in large tanks to meet 18 per cent of water needs.
- Visible water meters in the kitchen encourage people to use water more carefully.

Recycling

- Where possible, building materials come from renewable or recycled sources.
- A combined heat and power unit produces all the community's heat and electricity by burning waste.
- Recycled water (for example, dirty bath water) is used for toilets and garden watering.
- There are recycling bins in every home.

Transport

Reduce the need to travel
- Provides workspace and Internet connections to encourage residents to work at home and cut down on commuting.
- Shop, café and childcare facilities are provided in the community – helps to reduce journeys.
- An Internet link to a local supermarket with co-ordinated home deliveries reduces shopping trips.

Alternative to cars
- There are good public transport links in Beddington, including bus routes, railway stations and a tram link.
- Plenty of space for bike storage.
- On-site charging point for electric cars (as these become more popular).

▲ **E** How is BedZED sustainable?

Activities

1 What do you understand by the word *sustainable*?
   a) Write your own definition in pencil.
   b) Compare your definition with the meaning in the glossary at the back of this book. Which definition do you prefer? Write the best definition in pen.

2 Do you think BedZED would suit;
   a) a family with children?
   b) an older, retired couple?
   c) a young, single person?
   In each case give reasons.

Assignment

Design a sustainable home for your family to live in.
a) Draw plans (like the ones in D) or sketches to show your ideas for your home.
b) Annotate your plans or sketches to explain what makes your home sustainable.

TEST YOURSELF

I What is a settlement?

2 Describe three differences between an urban area and a rural area.

3 There are four possible sites to build a settlement in this drawing.

Key
River
Woodland
Marshland
Bridging point
(where it is possible
to build a bridge)
Possible settlement site

a) Choose the best site for a settlement.

b) Give three reasons for choosing this site.

4 a) Starting with the smallest, rank these settlements in order of size – town, city, hamlet, village.

b) Name one service found in each type of settlement that would not be found in a smaller settlement.

5 Are the following statements true or false? Correct any false statements.
- There are more small settlements than large ones.
- Small settlements are further apart than large ones.
- The larger a settlement the more services it provides.

6 Name three convenience goods and three comparison goods.

7 Label three areas on this transect of a city. The other one is done for you.

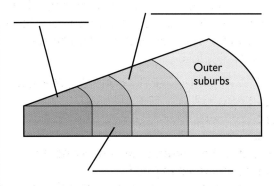

Outer suburbs

8 In which area of the city would you be most likely to:
a) go shopping for clothes?
b) live in an old house?
c) park your car in a garage?
In each case give a reason.

NOW, FOR A CHALLENGE!

9 Cities are always changing.

For a named case study, write a paragraph to describe either how the city changed in the past or how it is changing now.

10 How can cities become more sustainable places to live?

Either using a place you have studied or from your own personal experience, or both, explain how we could make cities more sustainable.

These are the words you should try to learn for this unit:

TOP TEN WORDS

*settlement   urban   rural   site
city   town   village   hamlet
convenience goods
comparison goods*

MORE KEY WORDS

*nucleated settlement
dispersed settlement
linear settlement   defensive site
market town   port   industrial town
resort   central business district (CBD)
inner city   suburb   inner suburb
outer suburb   terraced house*

IMPRESS YOUR TEACHER!

*function   transect
settlement hierarchy   conurbation
urban regeneration
sustainable living
ecological footprint   recycling*

UNIT 4

Economic Activity

▲ A British coal mine in the 1990s

▲ A modern call centre

Economic activities – or jobs – in Britain are changing. Many traditional activities, like coal mining, have almost disappeared. New activities, like work in call centres, have appeared in their place.

- What type of work did they do in coal mines? What do they do in call centres?
- Who is doing the work in each place? How is the workforce changing?
- From these photos, how would you say economic activities in Britain are changing?
- Are these changes good or bad, do you think? Why?

4.1   Fancy a job in football?

There is only one Wayne Rooney, but lots of teenagers dream of becoming a footballer (girls included – women's football is the fastest-growing sport in Britain). Unfortunately, only a few will make it. There are only about 5,000 professional footballers in England, for example.

But do not despair. Football is big business these days. There are thousands of other, football-related, jobs you could do, even if you don't become a footballer. Drawing B will give you some ideas.

▲ **A** Wayne Rooney – a football superstar

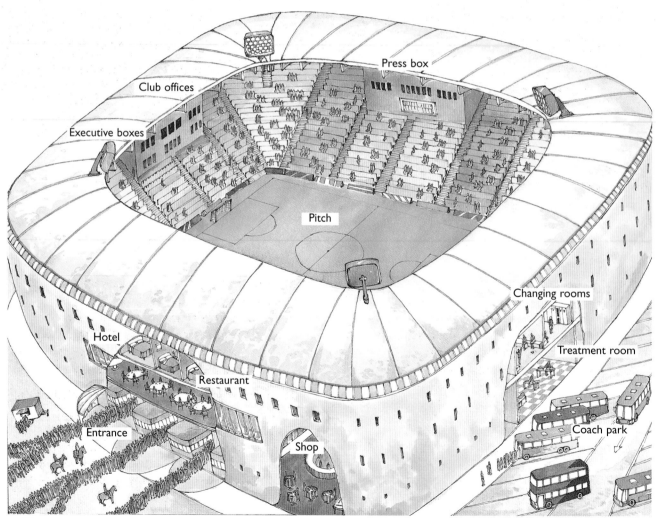

▲ **B** Match day at a football stadium. How many jobs can you find?

Football is a global economic activity. It is the world's most popular sport, played in every country. Perhaps the best-known league of all is the English Premier League. It is broadcast all around the world by satellite. The Premiership attracts some of the world's finest footballers. The top teams have players from every corner of the world (photo C). This is a good example of globalisation – the way that jobs, people and ideas move around the world.

| … from Portugal | … from England | … from Ukraine | … from Portugal | … from Germany | … from England |

| … from Ghana | … from France | … from England | … from Ivory Coast | … from Netherlands |

▲ **C** The Chelsea squad and some of the countries they come from

Activities

1 Look at picture B.
   a) Think of all the jobs that are done at a football club. List the jobs under each of the places labelled in the picture. For example, Club office – directors, accountants, secretaries … .
   b) Now, think of other jobs, connected with football, done elsewhere. Make another list. For example, Making the football shirts the players wear. Who can make the longest list?

2 Look at photo C. It doesn't matter if you don't know the players' names. If the photo is out of date, go to the Chelsea website at www.chelseafc.com to find the latest squad. Or choose your own team.

   a) Find the countries that the players come from on a world map in your atlas.
   b) Shade the countries on an outline map of the world and label them. Give the map a title.
   c) Describe the pattern on your map. Where do most of the players come from?

3 There are arguments for and against globalisation.
   a) Think of at least one argument for having foreign players in the Premiership.
   b) Think of at least one argument against. (You might be able to use similar arguments later when you think more about globalisation.)

4.2   Resources and economic activity

Everything we use, including the food we eat, comes originally from the natural environment. These are called natural resources. Wheat, fish, timber and oil are all natural resources. All products come from natural resources. For example, plastic is made from oil, bread is made from wheat, tables are made from wood. People obtain these natural resources by primary activities.

▲ **A** Farming

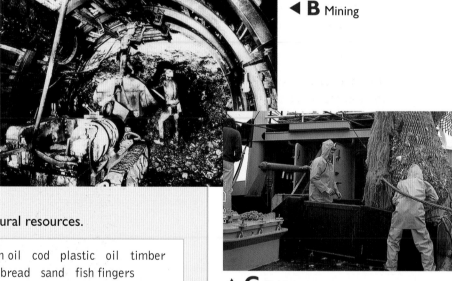

◀ **B** Mining

▲ **C** Fishing

Activities

1   Look at photos A–D, which show different primary activities in the UK. Which natural resources are obtained by each one?

2   Read the list of materials in the box below.
   a) Sort them into two groups – one of natural resources and one of products made from natural resources.

> glass   cotton   beer   wheat   palm oil   cod   plastic   oil   timber
> soap   chair   shirt   water   bread   sand   fish fingers

   b) Match each product with the natural resource that it comes from. Try the easy ones first, then see what's left.

▶ **D** Forestry

Primary activities are the way that people obtain raw materials. Farming, mining and fishing are primary activities.

Secondary activities are the way that people make or manufacture things from natural resources. This often happens in factories.

Tertiary activities are services. Doctors, teachers, bus drivers and footballers all provide services.

Quaternary activities are hi-tech services that provide information or expertise. Software design and biotechnology are quaternary activities.

3 Read the list of jobs in the box below. Sort them into primary, secondary, tertiary and quaternary activities.

> coal miner   pop singer   builder   baker
> fire fighter   logger
> television factory worker   fish farmer
> shoemaker   bus driver   nurse
> oil rig worker   police officer   car mechanic
> shop assistant   gardener   cleaner
> nursery nurse   call centre worker
> computer consultant   lawyer

4 a) Do a survey of people in your class to find out one job that a member of each person's family does. Sort the list into primary, secondary, tertiary and quaternary jobs.

Number of people

Primary   Secondary   Tertiary   Quaternary

b) Draw a bar chart to show the number of people involved in primary, secondary, tertiary and quaternary activities.
  What type of economic activity do most people in your area work in?

Homework

5 What are the main economic activities in your local area? If you don't know, do some research to find out. How does this help to explain the bar chart that you drew in 4b?

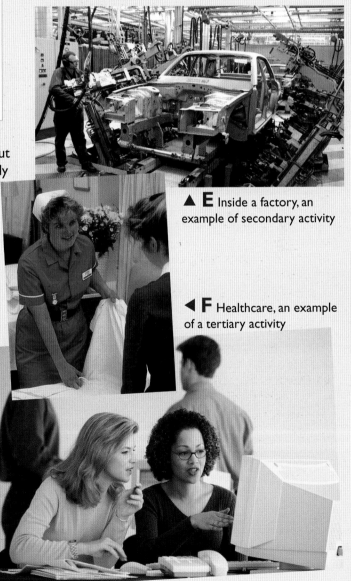

▲ **E** Inside a factory, an example of secondary activity

◀ **F** Healthcare, an example of a tertiary activity

▶ **G** IT consultancy, an example of a quaternary activity

4.3 Locations for manufacturing industry

Each economic activity has to find the best location. This may differ from one activity to another. Companies involved in manufacturing industry have to consider a number of factors before choosing a site for a factory.

> **Factors in choosing a location or site for manufacturing industry**
>
> - **Raw materials:** used to manufacture goods. Factories need to locate close to their raw materials if these are heavy or perishable.
> - **Power:** needed to make machinery work. In the past, this was likely to be water or coal, but today it's more likely to be electricity.
> - **Labour:** the workers needed to operate the machines. As technology changes, fewer people may be needed but they have to be better trained.
> - **Market:** the consumers who will buy the goods. The largest markets are usually urban areas where most people live.

▲ **A** Steelworks at Port Talbot, South Wales. Huge amounts of coal are used to heat iron ore to turn it into steel. Today, iron ore and coal are usually imported.

▲ **B** Sugar factory near Newark in the Midlands. Sugar beet is brought to the factory from nearby farms. The beet has to be processed soon after it is harvested.

▲ **C** A modern newspaper printing works. New technology allows newspapers to be printed at locations around the country. Newspapers have to be delivered by the next morning.

▲ **D** Workshop in northern England. The textile industry still employs many people. Factories and workshops depend on the skills of these workers.

▲ **E** Fleet Street, in London, was the home of most national newspapers

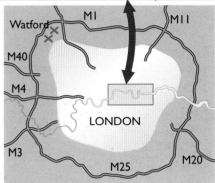

Key
× Modern printing works
▭ Fleet Street (original location of printworks)
— Roads   ●— Stations
═ Motorways   ⬭ Urban area

Another key factor in the location of industry is transport. Improvements in transport have led to some industries changing locations. Until the 1980s, most of the national daily newspapers in Britain were edited and printed around Fleet Street in central London. They were distributed by rail around the country. Congested roads in the city and overcrowded buildings were a major problem.

New technology now allows newspapers to edit and then print their papers at separate sites. By moving further from city centres, they were able to build new, larger printing works and gain better access to the new road network. Now, most newspapers are distributed by road.

▲ **F** Location of newspaper printing works in London

Activities

1 Study the information on the opposite page. Look at photos A–D. Which was the most important factor in choosing a location for each industry – raw materials, power, labour or market?

2 Look at drawing G on the right. Choose the best site on the drawing for each factory. In each case, write a sentence to explain your choice.

3 Look at the maps in F.
  a) Describe the changes in location of the newspaper industry in London since 1980.
  b) Compare photos C and E. What are the differences between the two sites?
  c) Explain why the location of the newspaper industry changed.

Homework

4 Find out about one manufacturing industry in your local area. Describe and explain its location. How long has it been there? Has its location changed? If so, why?

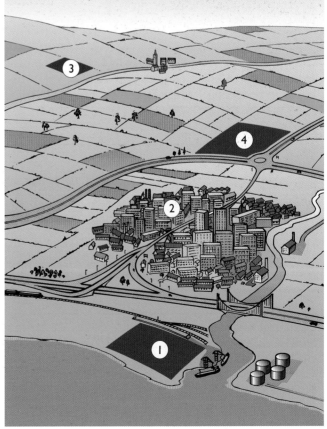

▲ **G** Possible sites for the factories in photos A–D

4.4   **Globalisation**

No matter where you go in the world these days, you'll come across the same familiar brand names (A). It's all part of globalisation. The names and logos belong to trans-national corporations – or TNCs for short – large companies that have branches in countries all around the world. Some of these corporations are so big that they are wealthier than the countries they operate in. Wal-mart, the world's biggest trans-national corporation, is wealthier than Denmark (table B)!

▲ **A** Spot the well-known brand names

Country/TNC (country where it is based in brackets)	GDP/sales in $ billions (wealth produced in a year by the country/TNC)
USA	11,712
Japan	4,623
UK	2,124
China	1,932
India	691
Sweden	346
Wal-mart Stores (USA)	288
BP (UK)	285
Exxon Mobil (USA)	271
Shell (UK/Holland)	269
Denmark	241
General Motors (USA)	193
Ireland	182
DaimlerChrysler (USA)	177
Toyota Motor (Japan)	173
Ford Motor (USA)	172
Thailand	162
General Electric (USA)	153
Total Fina Elf (France)	153
Malaysia	118

Activities

1 Look at the names and logos in A.
   a) How many can you recognise? Make a list.
   b) What does each one produce? For example, Coca-Cola produce fizzy drinks

2 Look at table B.
   a) Sort the list into two groups – countries and TNCs. Make two lists.
   b) Which is the richest country? Which is the richest TNC?
   c) In which countries are the top ten TNCs based? Suggest a reason for this.
   d) What does each TNC produce? (You'll know most of them, but some names are a clue.) What things appear often on your list?

◀ **B** League table of countries and top ten TNCs
Source: The Pocket World in Figures 2007

Globalisation means that the decisions you make affect people in other parts of the world. The fashion industry is a good example. Once upon a time our clothes were produced in factories here. Now, TNCs go all over the world to find the cheapest place to manufacture our clothes. Just look at the labels on your clothes if you don't believe it!

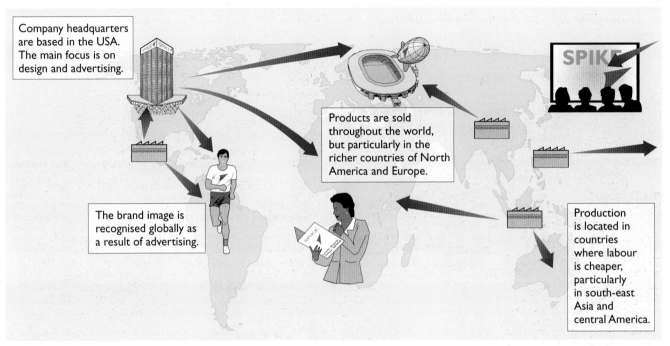

Company headquarters are based in the USA. The main focus is on design and advertising.

The brand image is recognised globally as a result of advertising.

Products are sold throughout the world, but particularly in the richer countries of North America and Europe.

Production is located in countries where labour is cheaper, particularly in south-east Asia and central America.

▲ **C** How the modern fashion industry works

3 Look at map C.
   a) Where are the clothes designed?
   b) Where are the clothes advertised and sold?
   c) Where are the clothes made?

4 Look at graph D.
   a) Where are the countries with the highest wages? Where are the countries with the lowest wages?
   b) How does this help to explain what you saw on map C?

5 a) Who do you think benefits most from globalisation:
    • shoppers in the UK?
    • workers who make the clothes?
    • TNCs who own the brand name?
   Explain your answer.
   b) And who do you think loses? Explain again.

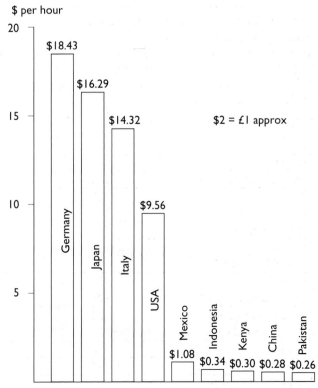

$ per hour

$18.43 Germany
$16.29 Japan
$14.32 Italy
$9.56 USA
$1.08 Mexico
$0.34 Indonesia
$0.30 Kenya
$0.28 China
$0.26 Pakistan

$2 = £1 approx

▲ **D** Wage rates for clothing workers in some countries

4.5

What work can you find in Reading?

In this case study you will identify different types of economic activity on an Ordnance Survey map of Reading, and find out why it is a good location for modern industry.

Reading is a fast-growing town in the south-east of England. It lies in the Thames Valley, 60 km west of London, in the so-called 'M4 Corridor'. It is one of the most prosperous regions in the country, with a range of economic activities where people find employment.

▲ **A** The brewery where Courage beer is made

▲ **B** A gravel pit where gravel is dug from the ground

▲ **C** The Madejski Stadium where Reading FC play

Activities

1 Look at photos A, B and C.
   a) For each photo, say whether it is an example of a primary, secondary or tertiary activity. In each case, give a reason.
   b) Match each photo with one of these grid references on map D:
   708 697   738 748   708 693

2 Look at map D. Find at least five other economic activities on the map.
   a) Name the place (e.g. hotel) and say whether it is a primary, secondary or tertiary activity.
   b) Give a six-figure grid reference for each place that you find.

3 A modern football stadium needs:
   • a large flat site for the stadium itself, and for car parking
   • a nearby town or city for its supporters
   • good transport links for people to get to matches easily.
   a) Look carefully at map D. Identify the factors that make the Madejski Stadium a good site for a stadium.

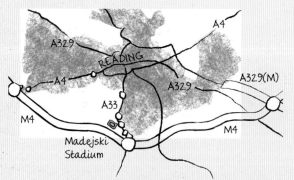

   b) Draw a large sketch map, like this, to show the location of the Madejski Stadium. Annotate your map to show why it is a good site for a football stadium.

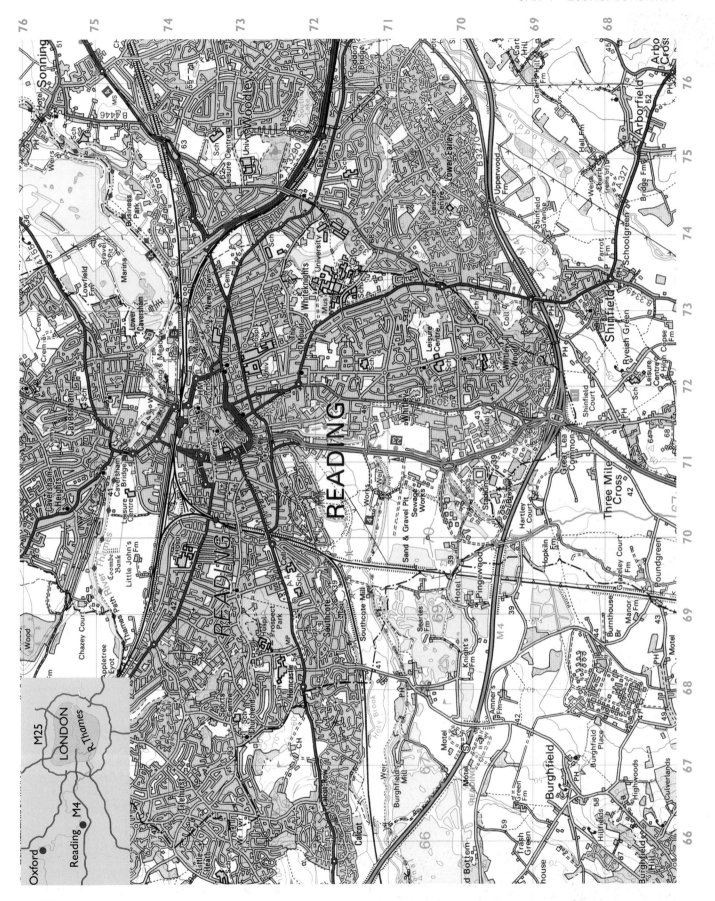

▲ **D** Reading. Reproduced from the 2006 1:50 000 Ordnance Survey map of Reading by permission of the Controller of HMSO © Crown Copyright.

What brings IT companies to Reading?

Reading, and the whole M4 Corridor, is an economic success story. Over the past twenty years it has attracted hundreds of new businesses and now boasts one of the biggest clusters of information technology (IT) companies in Europe. *Microsoft* (photo F), *IBM*, *Dell*, *Compaq* and *Fujitsu* are just some of the well-known IT companies in and around Reading.

Why Reading?

- The M4 connects Reading to London, Bristol and Wales. Via the M25 and M5, it is also connected to the rest of the UK and to Europe.
- It is also on the main Bristol–London rail line, 30 minutes from central London.
- It is close to Heathrow Airport, with good access to every part of the world.

- It has all the advantages of being close to London without the high costs of being in London.
- The region has a well-educated workforce, with the universities of Reading, Oxford, Bristol and Bath nearby.
- IT companies help to attract each other as they depend on the same services and skills. Workers can move easily from one company to another.
- The Chilterns and Downs provide an attractive environment for people to live and work.

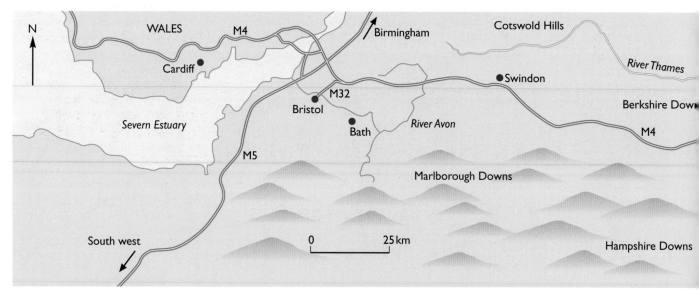

▲ **E** The M4 Corridor

Activities

1 Look at map E.
   a) Name the towns and cities close to the M4.
   b) Why do you think the region is called the 'M4 Corridor'?

2 Look at photo F.
   a) What type of economic activity is *Microsoft* involved with – primary, secondary, tertiary or quaternary? Give a reason for your answer.

   b) Find the location of *Microsoft's* UK Headquarters at grid reference 748 742, on map D on page 91. Describe the location on the map.
   c) Find Reading on map E. Describe its location on the map.
   d) Why is this a good location for *Microsoft*? Choose three reasons that you think would be most important for *Microsoft*.

▲ **F** *Microsoft's* UK Headquarters in Reading. *Microsoft* is an American TNC.

London
Office rent: £84 per sq ft
Average weekly pay: £556
Average house price: £307,000

Reading
Office rent: £24 per sq ft
Average weekly pay: £450
Average house price: £196,000

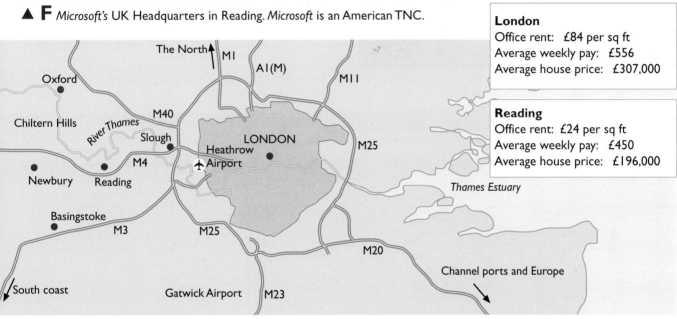

Assignment

Work with a partner.

You are the directors of a small, but growing, IT company that wants to move to Reading. You have to choose the best location for your new offices.

1 Find the three possible locations for your new offices on map D.
2 Decide which of the three locations you will choose.
3 Write a report to explain why you chose this location, but not the other two locations.

LOCATION A

727 737   One floor of a high-rise office block close to the centre of Reading. Rents are high. There are other companies in the block, including some IT companies.

LOCATION B

714 695   On a modern business park close to the edge of Reading. Rents are fairly high. There is plenty of room for car parking and it is in an attractive environment.

LOCATION C

675 681   On a new business park, soon to be built on a greenfield site near Reading. Rents are fairly low. There will be plenty of room for future expansion.

4.6   **Where should a new car plant be built?**

In this case study you will decide where a Japanese car company would choose to build a new manufacturing plant.

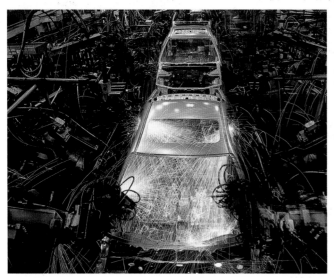

▲ **A** Japanese cars being made

Japan has been one of the most successful industrial countries over the past 50 years. Many Japanese products, from TVs to tumble driers, cameras to cars, are bought in Britain and other European countries. This is a threat to European companies.

The European Union (EU) was formed to increase trade within Europe. It tries to protect European companies from foreign competition by restricting the amount of imports from outside the EU. Japanese companies, keen to secure a share of the large European market, want to build their own factories in Europe.

▼ **B** Car assembly plants and densely populated areas in Europe

Key
• Car assembly plant
  Areas with highest population density

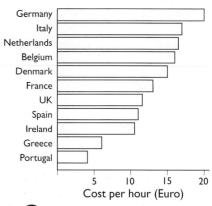

▲ **C** Labour costs in European countries

Activities

1 Work with a partner.
   You have been appointed by a Japanese car manufacturing company to find the best location in Europe to build a new car assembly plant. First, you need to decide in which country you should locate.
   a) Study the information on this page. The company is looking for:
   • A large market for its cars and also a good supply of labour. This means finding a densely populated area.

   • An experienced workforce and local supply of components. This means finding an area that already has a car industry.
   • Low labour costs.
   b) Choose the best country in which to locate. Use an atlas map to help you.
   c) Does any country meet all three requirements?
   d) Suggest the best area to locate in your chosen country. Give reasons.

The UK attracts many foreign companies, who want to invest here. One reason is that British wage rates are lower than some parts of Europe. The traditional centre of the British car industry is the Midlands, which has the lowest production costs (map E).

However, the government is keen to bring new industry to areas with high levels of unemployment. It identifies areas most in need of help as development areas. Other areas in need of help are intermediate areas. Companies that invest here are given grants and loans – up to 30 per cent of the cost of a new factory in a development area, and 20 per cent in an intermediate area.

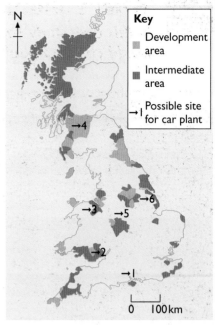

▲ **D** Assisted areas in Britain

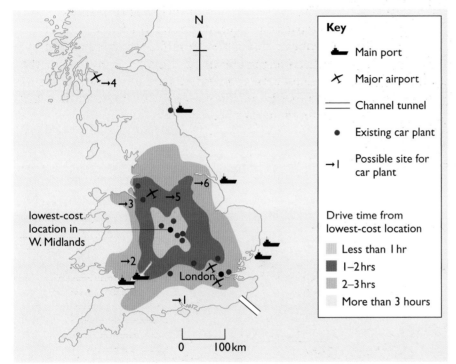

◀ **E** Costs of car production in Britain

2 Your company has decided to locate in the UK. The issue for you now is where in the UK?

   a) Study the information on this page. The company is looking for a site:
   - close to the lowest-cost location
   - close to a port
   - close to an airport
   - in an assisted area

   Decide which of the above requirements would be most important for a car plant in your view. Rank them in order of importance.

   b) Write them in this order on a copy of the table on the right, in the spaces at the top.

   c) Compare the possible sites on maps D and E. Complete the table, ticking the boxes that apply to each site. Write a score in each box you have ticked: 4 if it is in the second column, 3 in the

   third and so on. Add the total score for each location.

   d) Now choose the best site, using your table to explain why you chose it.

Site	x4	x3	x2	x1	Total score
1					
2					
3					
4					
5					
6					

Did Toyota make the right choice?

Toyota, Japan's biggest car company, decided to build their new car manufacturing plant at Burnaston, near Derby. Did you choose the same location in activity 2 on page 95? This was site 5 on the maps on the previous page. The plant opened in 1992 (photo F).

The Burnaston plant covers 235 hectares (about 400 football pitches).	It employs over 4,100 workers to assemble the cars.	It makes 285,000 cars every year; 85 per cent of them are exported, mainly to Europe.

It produces over 1,200 cars every 24 hours.	Total UK manufacturing investment by Toyota is over £1.75 billion.

▲ **F** Toyota's car plant at Burnaston

Activities

1 Look at photo F.
   a) Draw a large sketch, like this, of the Toyota car plant.
   b) Label features on your sketch that Toyota required when they were looking for a site in the UK. Choose the features from box G.

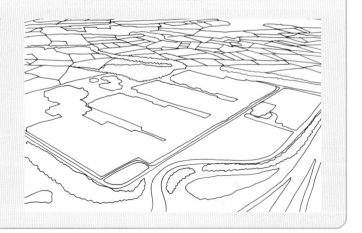

Since 1992 many car manufacturing plants in the UK have shut, or cut back on the number of cars they produce. Thousands of car workers have lost their jobs. This has not happened at Burnaston. The car plant has actually expanded production since it first opened.

- A large, flat site with space for future expansion.
- Firm, stable ground, suitable for building a large factory.
- Good road links to transport components and cars.
- Access by road to major ports to ship cars to Europe.
- A large, skilled workforce within easy travelling time of the plant.
- A pleasant environment for the workforce to enjoy leisure time.

▲ **G** Toyota's requirements for a UK site

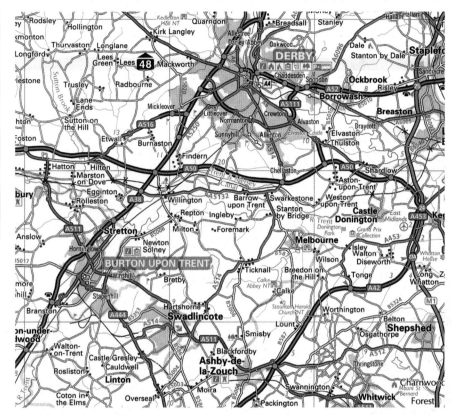

▲ **H** Extract from 1:160,000 road atlas map extract of the area around Burnaston © Automobile Association Developments Limited 2007 LIC003/07 A03397 © Crown copyright. All rights reserved. Licence number 100021153.

2 Look at map H.

a) Draw a large sketch map, like this, to show the location of the Toyota car plant.

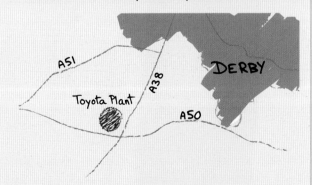

b) Label features on your map that Toyota required when they were looking for a site in the UK. Choose the features from box G.

Assignment

You have been asked to write a report for Toyota Head Office in Japan, to assess the choice of Burnaston as the site for their car plant in the UK. Your report should contain four sections:

1 Was the UK a good choice in Europe? (look at page 94)
2 Was Burnaston a good choice in the UK? (look at page 95)
3 Was the site a good choice? (look at pages 96–97)
4 Overall, has the car plant been a success?

4.7   What's the real price of a pair of jeans?

In this case study you will find out what part globalisation plays in the fashion industry, and consider whether this is good or bad.

Look at this pair of jeans. The label inside says, 'Made in Tunisia', but that's only part of the story. What the label does not tell you is the number of places that were involved in producing these jeans, or how far they have travelled. It is probably a similar story for the clothes you are wearing.

The jeans were designed in the UK.

The company that designed them is now owned by an American TNC.

The jeans were sewn together in a factory in Tunisia.

The zip was made in France using brass wire manufactured in Japan.

The cotton was grown in Benin.

The denim fabric was woven in Italy and dyed using dye made in Germany.

The jeans were stonewashed using pumice rock from Turkey.

The jeans were shipped to France, then on to the UK by lorry.

The brass rivets were made in Germany, with copper from Namibia and zinc from Australia.

Polyester fibre for the thread was made in Japan, using oil from Saudi Arabia.

Different types of thread were used. The thread was made in Northern Ireland (UK), Hungary and Turkey. It was dyed in Spain.

Soft cotton to line the pockets was grown and milled in Pakistan.

Finally, the jeans were sold in the UK.

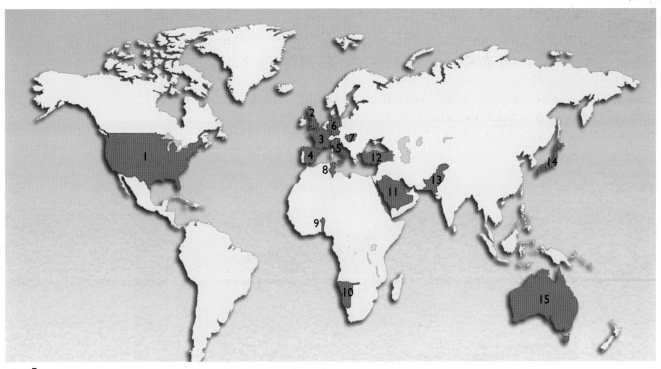

▲ **A** Countries involved in producing a pair of jeans

Activities

1 Look at map A. Shade the countries onto an outline map of the world.
   a) Name the countries numbered on the map. Write them in a key, e.g. 1=USA. You can check in an atlas.
   b) Describe how each country is involved in the production of a pair of jeans, e.g. Tunisia – the jeans were sewn together at a factory in Tunisia.

2 Draw a flow diagram to show all the stages in the production of a pair of jeans. You could start like this:

   Jeans sold in the UK

   Jeans shipped to France then by lorry to the UK

   Jeans sewn together in Tunisia, then stonewashed

   Pumice rock from Turkey

3 Look at pictogram B. If it costs £30 to buy a pair of jeans, how much money goes to:
   a) the shop that sells them?
   b) the company that manufactured them?
   c) the workers in the factory that made them?

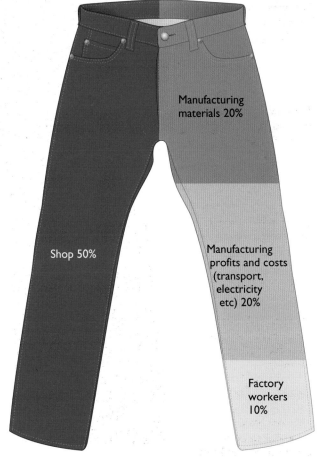

Manufacturing materials 20%

Shop 50%

Manufacturing profits and costs (transport, electricity etc) 20%

Factory workers 10%

▲ **B** Where the money goes for a pair of jeans

Who wins, who loses in global fashion?

In many poorer countries around the world, thousands of young women (it is usually women) work in factories to make our clothes (photo C). The labels in your clothes will tell you where they were made, but they will not tell you who made them. You will never meet the person who made your clothes. If you did, you might be shocked.

▲ **C** Women workers in a clothing factory

Ejallah Dousab is twenty-one. She works at a jeans factory in Ras Jebel, a small town in Tunisia, North Africa. When she was at school, Ejallah had other ambitions. However, there are three clothing factories in Ras Jebel and that is where most girls end up working.

The factory is really just a huge grey shed that, for most of the year, swelters under the hot, Mediterranean sun. Five hundred women work all day, amidst the heat and noise, without air-conditioning, sewing jeans to be sold in Britain.

Ejallah has worked at the factory for four years. She is a trained machinist. For that she is paid 220 dinars a month – about £110. The women work in production lines, each at their own sewing machine and each with their own part to play – zips, pockets, seams, hems. Ejallah concentrates hard, keeping her hands away from the pounding needle. There is no safety guard on the machine. If she slips it will pierce her finger. She grabs a pair of jeans from a trolley by her side, throws it onto her sewing machine, pushes it through and throws it back on the pile for the next job to be done. Over and over, keeping her eyes down and muscles clenched. By the end of the day they are aching.

Each line of workers has a target of 2,000 pairs of jeans a day. If they make their targets they get a bonus – 30 dinars, or £15 a month each. Work is from 7.15a.m. until noon, and then 1.p.m. until 5.45p.m., with an hour off for lunch. Workers have a maximum of two 15-minute toilet breaks. It takes at least that long to walk to the toilets and back.

Does Ejallah like her job? In front of her supervisor she say, "Yes, of course". Her family depends on the money she earns. But, one day, she thinks that she may get married and leave.

Ejallah's story is similar to millions of other clothing factory workers around the world. Many work in so-called **sweatshops**, for long hours, on low pay, in even worse conditions than Ejallah.

(Adapted from a true story in The Guardian newspaper.)

Source: The Story of the Blues, *The Guardian*, 2001

Companies involved in the global fashion industry search the world for factories that can produce clothes cheaply and reliably. The aim is to make as much profit as possible. So, to compete against other companies, they need to find the cheapest labour.

Some workers in poorer countries have joined together to protest about their wages and conditions they work in. Some shoppers in richer countries, like the UK, don't want to buy clothes if the workers are being exploited. There is a battle to change the fashion industry. But who has the real power?

▲ **D** The global fashion industry

Activities

1 Read Ejallah's story. Put yourself in her position. Should she give up or should she carry on doing the job?

a) Draw a picture of Ejallah, like this, in your book.

b) Think of reasons why she should give up or why she should carry on. List them beside your picture, under the two headings.

2 Study drawing D. Work out what might happen if …
a) … the TNC decided not to give the contract to the factory?
b) … the factory was making a loss on the contract it agreed to?
c) … factory workers went on strike for higher wages?
d) … shoppers refused to buy clothes because of how the company treated its workers?

3 Think about the global fashion industry.
a) Which group of people do you think has most power?
b) Which group do you think has the least power?
c) What power have you got? How could you use it to change the way the global fashion industry works?

Globalisation – good or bad?

From what you have learnt about the global fashion industry you might decide that it is best simply not to buy clothes made abroad. But it is not quite as simple as you might think.

Globalisation affects every area of our lives – fashion, food, football, whatever. There are arguments for and against.

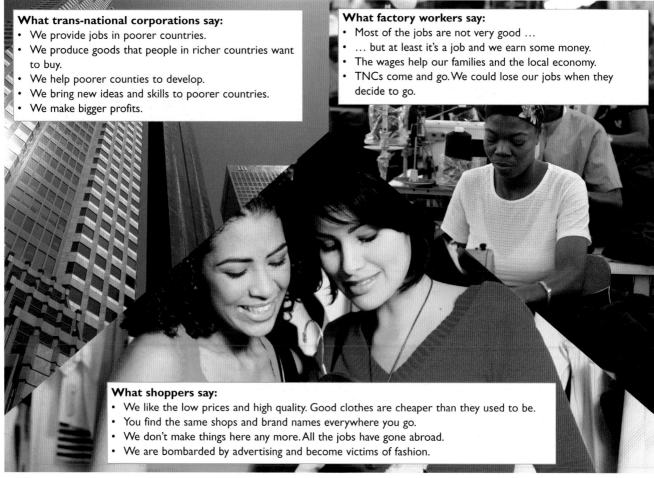

What trans-national corporations say:
- We provide jobs in poorer countries.
- We produce goods that people in richer countries want to buy.
- We help poorer counties to develop.
- We bring new ideas and skills to poorer countries.
- We make bigger profits.

What factory workers say:
- Most of the jobs are not very good …
- … but at least it's a job and we earn some money.
- The wages help our families and the local economy.
- TNCs come and go. We could lose our jobs when they decide to go.

What shoppers say:
- We like the low prices and high quality. Good clothes are cheaper than they used to be.
- You find the same shops and brand names everywhere you go.
- We don't make things here any more. All the jobs have gone abroad.
- We are bombarded by advertising and become victims of fashion.

▲ **E** For or against globalisation?

Activities

1 Read all the comments about globalisation in E.
   a) Cut out copies of the comments and sort them into two groups – for and against globalisation.
   b) Draw a table like this in your book. Stick the comments under the correct heading in the table.

Arguments for globalisation	Arguments against globalisation

2 You are the President of a poorer country. Poorer countries are often called less economically developed countries or LEDCs.
   a) Identify the important arguments for *and* against globalisation for your country.
   b) Would you encourage TNCs to invest in your country, or not? Give the main reason.

3 Write a short speech for *or* against globalisation. Use any of the ideas on this page, plus your own ideas. You could make your speech as part of a debate in your class.

Whether you think globalisation is good or bad, it is impossible to stop it. What we can do is to make it fairer. There is an alternative mode of trading termed Fairtrade.

You can recognise Fairtrade certified products in the shop if they carry the FAIRTRADE Mark. The Mark guarantees:
- a fair and stable price for disadvantaged producers
- the opportunity for these producers to improve their lives
- greater respect for the environment
- closer links between shoppers and producers.

Guarantees a **better deal** for Third World Producers

FAIRTRADE ®

One small company involved in the fair trade fashion industry is called Hug.

Small-scale cotton farmers in Peru receive a guaranteed price for their cotton. They also receive an additional amount of money called a premium, which helps them invest in their future. (This picture shows a farmer in India who grows cotton for sale to Fairtrade retailers in the UK.)

The cotton is made into clothes in a factory in Peru. The factory works towards providing better working conditions and pay for its workers. (This picture shows workers in Egypt producing Hug clothing.)

You can buy the clothes with a clear conscience, knowing the disadvantaged farmers have benefited from a fairer price. (This picture shows the director of Hug's son modelling Hug clothing.)

Activity

Find out more about Hug by going to their website, www.hug.co.uk.

How does the way that they produce their clothes differ from the clothes produced by a typical TNC?

Assignment

Hug have called you in as an advertising consultant to help them to advertise a new range of jeans made from Fairtrade certified cotton.

Use all the ideas in this unit to help you to design an advert, explaining to shoppers why it is important they buy these jeans made from Fairtrade cotton.

TEST YOURSELF

1 Which of these people in your school is doing an economic activity?
a teacher   a cleaner   a pupil   a headteacher?
(you can choose more than one)
Explain your answer.

2 a) List six different jobs at a football club.
  b) List another two jobs, connected with football but done elsewhere.

3 Sort the following jobs into primary, secondary, tertiary or quaternary activities:

> firefighter   farmer   plumber   IT consultant
> footballer   car assembly worker

4 Name four factors to consider when choosing the site for a new factory.

5 a) Choose the best site for a new steelworks on this map.
  b) Give two reasons for choosing this site.

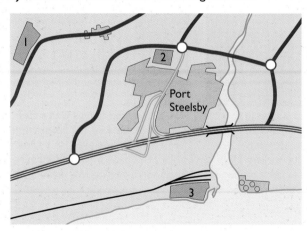

6 a) What is a trans-national corporation?
  b) Name three well-known TNCs that you have heard of.

7 The global fashion industry is a good example of globalisation.
  a) Name two countries where many of our clothes are made these days.
  b) Explain why companies make the clothes in these countries.

8 What do you think each of these people might think about globalisation? Complete a thought bubble for each person.

The head of a TNC   A clothing factory worker in Asia   A shopper in the UK

NOW, FOR A CHALLENGE!

9 How is the distribution of economic activities changing?
  Using a named case study, write a paragraph to describe how the distribution of one economic activity is changing, and why.

10 Globalisation – good or bad?
  Either write two paragraphs or complete a table to outline the benefits and problems of globalisation. Then, write a conclusion to give your own opinion.

These are the words you should try to learn for this unit:

> ### TOP TEN WORDS
> economic activity   primary activity
> secondary activity   tertiary activity
> quaternary activity   employment
> unemployment   natural resources
> globalisation
> trans-national corporation (TNC)

> ### MORE KEY WORDS
> manufacturing industry   raw material
> power   market   labour   transport
> distribution   call centre

> ### IMPRESS YOUR TEACHER!
> European Union   development area
> intermediate area
> less economically developed
> country (LEDC)
> more economically developed country
> (MEDC)   fair trade

UNIT 5

Environmental Issues

▲ Mentawi tribesman in the rainforests of Indonesia

People live in the tropical rainforest in Indonesia. They have a sustainable lifestyle. They know how to use the forest without destroying it.

- How would you describe the tropical rainforest that you can see in this photo?
- In what ways might this person make use of the forest?
- Why do you think that this lifestyle is sustainable?
- Do you think that your lifestyle is sustainable or not?
- Why do you think this?

5.1 Conflict in the park!

Most of us live in towns and cities. We share the same environment. On a nice day everybody goes to the park.

Just look at the park today – there are so many people (drawing A). People means crowds – and that can lead to conflict! Everyone's doing different activities and getting in each other's way. The only way to solve the problem is to manage what happens in the park.

Edna sits and looks at the flowers. She enjoys the fresh air.

Danny and his friends play football. Other kids join in.

Jim walks his dog every morning and evening.

Sally runs a boat-hire business. People row her boats on the lake.

Ghita jogs in the park. It's safer than running on the street.

Ron goes fishing. He likes peace and quiet ... and so do the fish!

▲ **A** Activities in the park

Activity

I Look at cartoon A. Read about the people who use the park. Then complete a conflict grid, like this.

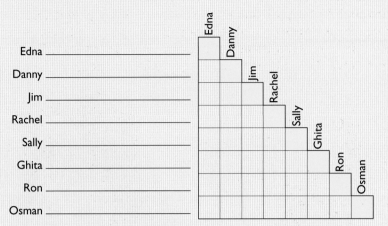

a) For each person, write what activity they do in the park on a large copy of the grid. For example, *Edna – sits and looks at flowers.*

b) Put a ✗ in each square where you think two activities are in conflict (have a negative effect on each other). For example, *plays football* and *sits and looks at flowers.* Put a ✓ in each square where you think the activities are in harmony (have a positive effect on each other). Put a 0 where they have no effect on each other. You should complete all the blank squares on the grid.

c) Choose one square where you put a ✗. Explain what the conflict is. Choose one square where you put a ✓. Explain why the activities are in harmony.

d) Overall, which activity do you think is most in conflict with other activities in the park? Which activity do you think is least in conflict?

2 Charlie is the park-keeper. His job is to manage what happens in the park to prevent any conflict between the activities and to protect the environment. It is a difficult job!

Here are some of the strategies that Charlie could try to manage the park:

- Ban some activities in the park altogether
- Fence off some areas in the park to be used for a single activity
- Put notices around the park with rules about how to behave, e.g. *keep off the grass*
- Let everybody do what they want and hope for the best

a) For each strategy, say whether you think it is a good one or not. Give reasons.

b) Write a short plan, about one paragraph, to help Charlie to manage the park. You could also draw a map to show your ideas.

Rachel brings her children to feed the ducks.

Osman sells ice cream from his van. Lots of customers in the park!

5.2 National Parks

A national park is different from a local park in a town or city. It is a large area of beautiful countryside that is protected by law. National parks have three main aims:

- to conserve the beauty, wildlife and heritage (history) of the area
- to help visitors find out about the area and enjoy it
- to meet the needs of people living in the area for homes and jobs.

National parks cover about 10 per cent of England and Wales (satellite photo A).

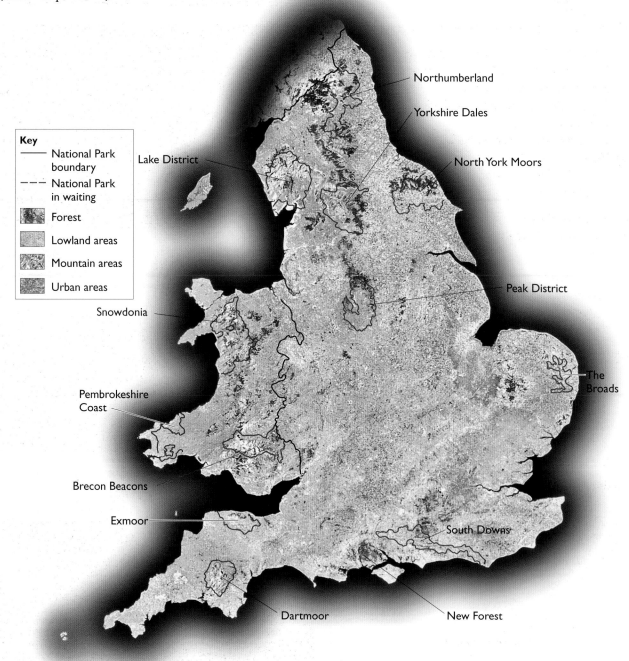

Key
— National Park boundary
--- National Park in waiting
▨ Forest
▨ Lowland areas
▨ Mountain areas
▨ Urban areas

Northumberland
Yorkshire Dales
North York Moors
Lake District
Peak District
Snowdonia
The Broads
Pembrokeshire Coast
Brecon Beacons
Exmoor
South Downs
Dartmoor
New Forest

▲ **A** Satellite photo of England and Wales showing the national parks

Activities

I Look at satellite photo A.

a) How many national parks are there in England and Wales?

b) Name one national park:
   i)   in a mountainous area
   ii) in a lowland area
   iii) on the coast
   iv) with forest
   v)   in waiting (soon to become a national park)

c) Which is the nearest national park to you?

2 a) Describe the distribution of national parks in England and Wales. You could write two sentences starting like this:
   Most of the national parks in England and Wales are ....
   There are fewer national parks in ....

b) How easy would it be to visit a national park if you lived in London? Explain why.
   How about if you lived in Manchester?

3 Look at the photos in B.

a) Identify the following features in each of the photos.

> farming   forest   moorland
> shops and services   housing   reservoir
> footpaths   village   mining   roads

b) Draw a Venn diagram with three circles like the one below. Label the circles as shown. Think about which features would be important for *recreation*, *conservation* and the *local community*. Write the features in the correct circle. Some features may appear in more than one circle where they overlap.

Recreation   **Conservation**

Local community

▲ **B** National Park scenes

5.3   Protecting the rural environment

Conservation is the way that we protect the environment.

In the UK, all sorts of people are involved in conservation, from the government, who decides which areas to protect and makes the laws, down to local voluntary groups, who do jobs like clearing footpaths and restoring ponds. In between the government and local voluntary groups is a range of other organisations like the National Trust, the Royal Society for the Protection of Birds (RSPB) and Friends of the Earth. Most of them depend on donations and volunteers to keep them going. Do you feel strongly about the environment? If you don't already belong to one of these organisations then perhaps you could get involved.

The government has established areas where the environment is protected. Can you recognise the four types of protected area in photos A-D?

- National parks are large areas of beautiful countryside where people go for recreation, but where other people still live and work.
- Heritage Coasts are stretches of beautiful coastline that are protected in a similar way to national parks.
- Environmentally Sensitive Areas are areas where the beauty of the landscape depends on maintaining traditional farming methods.
- Nature reserves are small areas where plants and animals need to be protected from human activities that could disturb, or destroy, them.

▲ A

▲ C

▲ B

▲ D

The main rural activity is still farming. Traditional farming methods created habitats where many types of wildlife thrived. Birds like the skylark used to be common in the UK. The skylark nests in crops and grass during the summer. Modern farming methods destroy suitable nesting sites. Source E shows that early harvesting of winter-sown crops and regular cutting of grass for silage disturbs the skylark during its nesting period. As a result its population has fallen by 60 per cent over the past 25 years. The loss of birds from the countryside has become a big worry for conservationists.

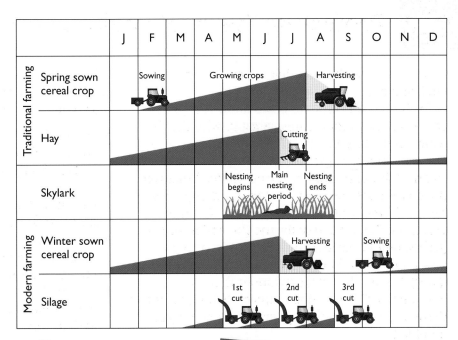

		J	F	M	A	M	J	J	A	S	O	N	D
Traditional farming	Spring sown cereal crop		Sowing			Growing crops				Harvesting			
	Hay							Cutting					
	Skylark					Nesting begins	Main nesting period	Nesting ends					
Modern farming	Winter sown cereal crop							Harvesting		Sowing			
	Silage					1st cut		2nd cut		3rd cut			

▲ **E** How traditional and modern farming methods affect the skylark

▶ **F** A skylark

Activities

1 You are going to complete a large table to compare four types of protected area.

  a) Match photos A–D to one type of protected area. In the first column of your table, list the letters A–D and, in the next column, write the types of protected areas.

Photo	Type of protection	Description	Why protect it?
A			

  b) In the third column, write a sentence to describe the environment in each photo.

  c) In the final column, suggest why each environment should be protected.

2 Study source E.

  a) Explain how modern farming methods have reduced the number of skylarks.

  b) How would a change back to traditional farming methods help skylarks to survive?

Homework

3 Do some research about one organisation involved in conservation. Find out what its aims are and what it does. The quickest way to do this would be on its website, using the internet. You can choose from this list, or find a local organisation.

- World Wide Fund for Nature (WWF) www.wwf-uk.org/
- The National Trust www.nationaltrust.org.uk
- Royal Society for the Protection of Birds (RSPB) www.rspb.co.uk
- British Trust for Conservation Volunteers (BTCV) www.btcv.org
- Greenpeace www.greenpeace.org
- Friends of the Earth www.foe.org.uk

Share the information with your class. You could choose one of these organisations to get involved with, either individually or as a class.

5.4   The rainforest ecosystem

Tropical rainforest is one of the world's natural ecosystems. It covers about 7 per cent of the world's land surface – an area about the size of the USA. Tropical rainforest has a huge variety of plant and animal species. An area of just one hectare is likely to have over a hundred species of tree. The same area of rainforest would also be home to hundreds of species of birds and fish, as well as many thousands of insects. Each of these plants and animals is uniquely adapted to the hot, wet environment of the rainforest.

Scientists believe that thousands of rainforest plants and animals have yet to be identified. If you were ever lucky enough to explore an area of rainforest, you might even be able to find a new species and have it named after you! Of course, many rainforest plants like bananas, rubber and pineapples have been known, and used, for a long time. In recent years other important discoveries have been made – such as the rosy periwinkle which is used as a treatment for people with leukaemia, a blood disease. No one knows what other valuable secrets the rainforest may contain.

▲ **A** Inside the tropical rainforest in Cameroon

Activities

1 Look at photo A.
   a) Identify each of the following features in the photo:

   > large evergreen leaves
   > tall straight tree trunks
   > wide buttress roots growing above ground
   > little undergrowth on forest floor
   > lianas (creepers) climbing up trees

   b) Draw a labelled sketch of the photo to show these features.

2 **a)** Read the five facts about rainforests below:
   - The forest is dark.
   - Plants grow upwards to reach light.
   - There is no winter, so the plants do not shed their leaves.
   - The Sun is overhead.
   - The soil is shallow.

   How do these facts help to explain the features labelled in your sketch?
   b) Match each feature with one fact. Now write a sentence about each pair to explain how plants have adapted to the rainforest environment. For example, *plants have evergreen leaves because there is no winter, so the plants do not shed their leaves.*

▲ **B** Cross-sectional view of rainforest

It is hard to imagine what it is like to be in a tropical rainforest unless you have experienced it for yourself. If you have ever been in a sauna, you will have some idea of how hot and sticky it is. However, it would give you no idea of the colour, the noise, or all the variety of living things.

Photo B, on the left, might look rather like other forests you have seen, until you realise the scale. The tallest emergent trees can grow to over 50 metres, the height of a ten-storey block of flats. The main canopy of the forest is about 30 metres, half as tall again as a typical British oak tree. Few plants grow on the dark forest floor, but near clearings and river banks dense undergrowth grows to about ten metres, higher than a double-decker bus!

3 a) Draw a cross-section of the rainforest, like the one on the right. Label three layers: emergent trees, main canopy and undergrowth. Give your drawing a vertical scale to show the height of the plants.
  b) On the same page, and at the same scale, draw:
   i) a double-decker bus
   ii) a typical British oak tree
   iii) a ten-storey block of flats.

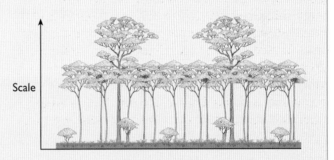

Scale

'You'll find the high spot of your day,' said the major, 'is cleaning your teeth. The only bit of you you can keep clean. Don't shave in the jungle, because the slightest nick turns septic at once. And don't take more than one change of clothes, because you must keep your weight well down. Keep one set of dry kit in a sealed bag in your pack. Get into that each night after you've eaten. Powder yourself all over, too, with zinc talc – you'll have half the rashes and the rot and the skin fungus. Then sleep. Then get up at five thirty and into your wet kit. It's uncomfortable at first, but don't weaken – ever; if you do, there'll be two sets of wet kit in no time, you'll lose sleep and lose strength and then there'll be a disaster. But take as many dry socks as you can.

Stuff them into all the crannies in your pack. And, in the morning, soak the pair you are going to wear in insect repellent, to keep the leeches out of your boots. Stick it on your arms and round your waist and neck and in your hair while you're about it. Cover yourself at night, too, against the mosquitoes. Take them seriously, because malaria is a terrible thing and it's easy to get, pills or no.'

▲ **C** From *Into the Heart of Borneo*, by Redmond O'Hanlon

4 Imagine that you are going on a journey through the rainforest. Make a list of all the things that you would take. Give a reason for taking each item. Extract C will give you some ideas, but use your imagination as well. Remember to keep the weight down – only take essential items.

Homework

5 It is important that you get permission from your parents before you do this activity. Never go alone.
  a) Choose any local ecosystem – woodland, meadow, park or wasteland.
  b) Carry out a plant survey over a small area (perhaps 10 m x 10 m, or larger if there are trees). Your teacher can give you more information about how to do this.
How many different species can you count? How would this compare with a tropical rainforest?

5.5 Do we need another national park?

In this case study you will examine the pressures for a new national park in the south-east of England. You will produce your own plan to show how you could manage one area of the park.

The South Downs is the latest national park to be proposed for England and Wales. Most of our national parks date back to the 1950s and are located in the north or west of the country. In contrast, the South Downs is in the south-east of England, just one hour from London by road or rail (map A). It stretches from the white chalk cliffs at Beachy Head (photo B) across Sussex and Hampshire to the historic town of Winchester.

The South Downs get their name from the rolling chalk downlands that form some of the best-known hills in Britain. However, this environment is under threat. Thirty-four million people visit the South Downs each year. It also has Britain's most popular long-distance footpath (the South Downs Way). Urban development along the south coast puts extra pressure on the Downs, for building new roads, shopping centres and even a new football stadium. As a national park, the South Downs will get better protection from these threats.

▼ **A** The South Downs

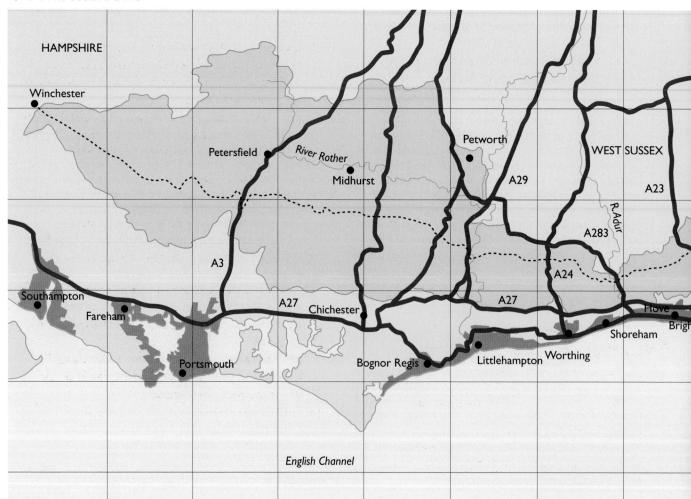

▲ **B** The Downs near Beachy Head

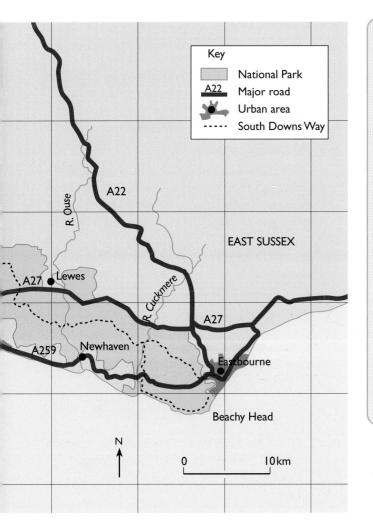

Key

National Park
A22 Major road
Urban area
- - - - South Downs Way

R. Ouse

A22

EAST SUSSEX

A27 Lewes

R. Cuckmere

A27

A259 Newhaven

Eastbourne

Beachy Head

N

0   10km

Activities

1 Look at map A. Work out the size of the proposed South Downs National Park.
   a) Measure the distance of the park from east to west using the scale on the map.
   b) Estimate the area of the park by counting the number of squares it fills on the map. (Each square on the map is 100 km^2).

2 Look at photo B.
   Draw a labelled sketch to show these features:

   > chalk cliffs   chalk downland (grass)
   > long-distance footpath   farmland   road
   > Beachy Head lighthouse

3 Answer these questions, using evidence from photo B.
   a) Why do you think people come to visit this area?
   b) How is the chalk downland under threat?
   c) Do you think that the Downs needs to be protected? Give reasons.

What conflicts are there on the South Downs?

Chalk downland is a unique ecosystem. It contains a rich variety of grasses and small flowering plants, including some that are found nowhere else (photo C). You could find up to 45 plant species in any square metre of downland.

Although chalk downland looks completely natural, it still has to be managed. Otherwise, it would soon become overgrown and turn into forest. Downland grows on thin, chalky soil that is not much good for growing crops, but it is good for grass. Sheep grazing on the grass help to prevent the growth of larger plants. Too many sheep (or people!) trampling on the Downs would wear down the grass and, eventually, erode the soil too (diagram D). This is what happens on a footpath when too many people use it.

▲ **C** Bee orchid – a rare plant found in chalk downland

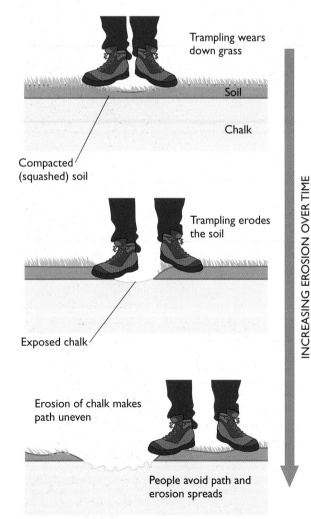

▲ **D** Erosion of a footpath on chalk downland

Trampling wears down grass

Soil

Chalk

Compacted (squashed) soil

Trampling erodes the soil

Exposed chalk

Erosion of chalk makes path uneven

People avoid path and erosion spreads

INCREASING EROSION OVER TIME

Activities

1 Look at diagram D.
   a) Write three sentences to explain how trampling on the Downs can damage the ecosystem. Use the three drawings to help you.
   b) What is the conflict between *conservation* (protecting the environment) and *recreation* (people enjoying the environment)?

2 Look at photo E.
   Complete a large conflict grid, like this, to show the conflicts and benefits between different land uses in the South Downs. (Use the example of a conflict grid on page 107 to help you.)

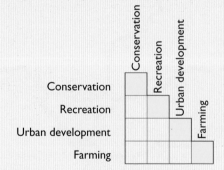

3 a) Describe one of the conflicts you can see in photo E.
   b) Which land use should take priority in a national park, do you think? Give reasons. (Look back to the national park aims on page 108.)

Conservation

The South Downs needs to be managed to protect the chalk downland landscape. Sheep graze the grass to prevent the growth of larger plants. Notice how shrubs have started to grow on the steeper slopes where the sheep don't graze.

I'm no ordinary sheep. I'm a landscape manager!

Urban development

Urban areas close to the South Downs are expanding as their population grows. The proposed site for Brighton and Hove Albion's (nicknamed the 'Seagulls') new football stadium is on the South Downs because there is no space for it in the town.

Do they mean us?

Come on you Seagulls!

Recreation

The South Downs are popular with walkers, mountain bikers and hang gliders. Most of the visitors concentrate at a few popular sites, like Beachy Head. Large numbers can lead to problems like litter, traffic congestion and erosion.

No congestion up here!

Farming

Over the years farmers have changed the South Downs. They have added fertiliser to the soil and replaced the grass with crops. Trees and hedgerows have been chopped down to make fields larger. So, today, there is less chalk downland.

This was home last year.

Now where do we go?

▲ **E** Conflicting land uses in the South Downs

How can the Downs be managed sustainably?

The Seven Sisters Country Park is one of the most popular places in the South Downs. It attracts over half a million visitors each year. (A country park is much smaller than a national park. There are hundreds of country parks around Britain.)

The country park contains a large area of chalk downland and a variety of other environments. The Cuckmere River has cut through the chalk to form a wide river valley (photo F). The sea has eroded the rolling hills of the Downs to form the Seven Sisters (seven large chalk cliffs in photo G). With so many visitors, the country park needs to be managed sustainably to conserve the environment, so future generations can also enjoy it.

Lagoon formed behind the beach, attracts birds

Grazing marsh formed on river flood plain

Cuckmere River

◄ F The Cuckmere Valley

Chalk downland

Rocky shore

Shingle beach

► G The Seven Sisters cliffs

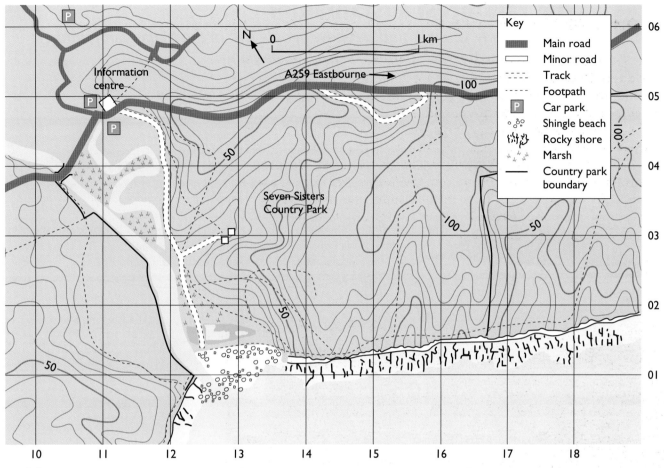

▲ **H** Seven Sisters Country Park

Activity

Look at photos F and G.

Find each of the environments labelled on the photos on map H. Give a four-figure grid reference for a square where you would find each one. For example, *chalk downland in square 1303*.

Assignment

You are going to produce a management plan for the Seven Sisters Country Park. The plan should have two main aims:

- to conserve the natural beauty and wildlife in the park
- to encourage people to understand and enjoy the park.

On a large copy of map H, divide the park into two zones:

Active zone where people can do a variety of activities like cycling, picnicking and swimming.

Wild zone where natural beauty and wildlife are conserved and no activities are allowed. People can walk there.

You can make the zones any size or shape you want, depending on how you think the park should be managed. Think carefully about where the zones should be located. Mark them onto your copy of the map.

Write a short report to explain the decisions that you made.

5.6   Is the rainforest sustainable?

In this case study you will find out how people live in the Malaysian rainforest and decide how the forest could be used sustainably.

> My name is Evelyn. I am an Iban. We live in the forests of Sarawak – part of the island of Borneo that belongs to Malaysia. Our people have always lived here, far away from cities and other modern influences. But our life is changing. Today, it is a mixture of our old traditions and modern ways copied from the outside world.
> The whole of our community – about 180 people – lives in a longhouse surrounded by rainforest. We still survive by hunting, fishing and farming. But these days we also wear trainers, play football and watch TV.

▲ **A**

▲ **C** Location of Nanga Sumpa

▲ **B** The Nanga Sumpa longhouse in Sarawak, home to 180 people

People have lived sustainable lives in the rainforests of Borneo for hundreds of years. The majority of Iban people in rural Borneo still live in longhouses. Traditionally, the longhouse was built entirely from forest materials. These days other materials are used as well. The Nanga Sumpa longhouse is about 100 metres long and 10 metres wide. It is built mainly from timber with a corrugated iron roof. It stands about four metres off the ground on bamboo stilts. Sometimes, animals are kept under the building.

Everybody in the community lives in the longhouse. One side is divided into thirty private family apartments. On the opposite side is an open veranda — like a long porch — with steep wooden steps down to the ground.

A large communal area runs down the centre of the longhouse. This is used daily for meetings, craftwork, dancing and drumming — all important in Iban life. Sometimes a net containing smoked, dried human heads hangs from the roof of the communal area — a reminder of the days when the Iban were head-hunters. But today you are just as likely to see posters of your favourite pop star or football team!

▲ **D** Inside the longhouse

Activities

1 Study all the information on pages 120–21.

Make two lists of the features of Iban lifestyle under the headings *traditional* and *modern*.

The Iban people use the land around the longhouse for farming. Each small field is used for just two or three years and then left fallow for up to fifteen years. The Iban make new fields by chopping down the forest and burning it. They leave the ash on the ground to make it fertile.

In the past, because the soil quickly lost its fertility, the Iban soon had to move on to new ground. But these days it is common to find chemical fertilisers being used so that new land does not have to be cleared so often.

The Iban grow hill rice, sweetcorn, peppers and palms for oil as their main crops. They also fish in the River Ai and travel into the forest to collect fruits and hunt for meat. The Iban have a well-balanced diet which means that they live long lives. Until recently, their way of life had remained unchanged for hundreds of years without having much harmful impact on the rainforest environment. Even the land they cleared and then later abandoned grew back into forest.

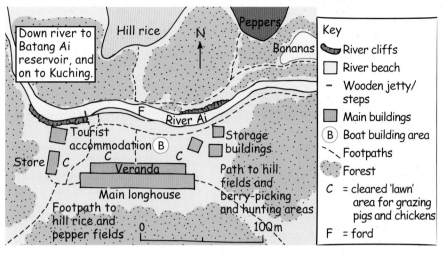

▲ **E** Sketch map of Nanga Sumpa in Sarawak, Borneo

▶ **F** Women wash in the river while men repair an outboard motor

▶ **G** Clearing the forest to grow crops

2 a) Using the descriptions on page 120, draw a plan of a typical longhouse. Give your plan a scale.
  b) Think of the advantages and disadvantages of living in a home like this. Write them down in a table under these two headings.

3 Think about the traditional farming methods of the Iban.
  a) Why was this method sustainable for so long?
  b) How have farming methods changed recently? Will this make farming more or less sustainable, do you think?

Homework

4 Compare your own lifestyle with that of the Iban people.

Think about the similarities as well as the differences in the two lifestyles. Include the following headings in your comparison:
• Diet   • Transport
• Housing   • Clothing
• Leisure

Whose lifestyle do you think is more sustainable?

How is the rainforest changing?

Our community really began to change when they built the dam at Batang Ai, further down the River Ai. Until then, it used to take about three days for us to reach the nearest town along the river. Now the journey can be done in half a day with the help of outboard motors on our canoes. We are less isolated than we were. That means there is more trade and tourism. There is still no road here though. The people who lived near the dam were not so lucky. Their homes were flooded by the new lake and so was the forest.

▼ **H** Map of SW Sarawak, including the area around Nanga Sumpa

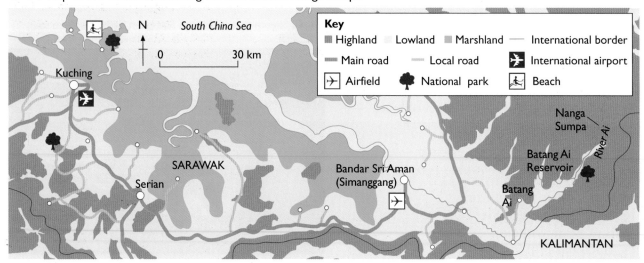

BORNEO EXPERIENCE

Experience a three-day trip to a genuine Iban longhouse.

DAY 1 Depart from luxury air-conditioned hotel in Kuching at 6a.m. Six-hour bus journey to Batang Ai Reservoir. You will then be taken by canoe, navigated by your Iban hosts, on a four-hour trip upstream to the Nanga Sumpa longhouse. You will be greeted on arrival with a huge meal, followed by a party well into the night. This is part of traditional Iban hospitality and your arrival is a good excuse for a party!

DAY 2 Wake before dawn when the longhouse comes to life, and spend a typical day with the Iban. You will be invited to share all meals. Do eat as much as you can – this is considered good manners. You will also be expected to bathe in the river at the beginning and end of the day as a way of keeping clean. The water is quite safe. For the rest of the day you will be able to observe the people at their daily tasks – weaving, boat-building, farming and fishing.

DAY 3 Return to Kuching for a well-deserved rest and a good shower!

◀ **I** A tourist brochure

Activities

1 On map H find Nanga Sumpa.
   a) Work out the distance, by river and road, to Kuching. Why do you think that the road stops at Batang Ai?
   b) Explain how building the dam has made the village more accessible.

2 Read tourist brochure I.
   a) Is this the sort of experience you would enjoy if you were on holiday in Borneo? Give your reasons.
   b) Suggest what impact tourism could have on the Iban people.
      • Will it bring any benefits or problems?
      • How will it change their way of life?

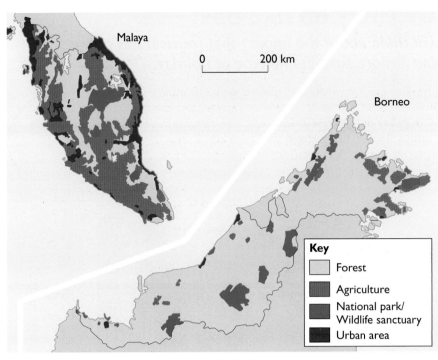

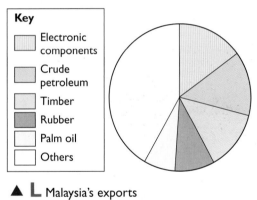

Malaya

Borneo

0   200 km

Key

☐ Forest

▨ Agriculture

▨ National park/
   Wildlife sanctuary

■ Urban area

▲ **J** Land use in Malaysia

Over 70 per cent of Malaysia is covered by forest. This area is rapidly shrinking. Malaysia is a newly industrialised country (NIC) and tropical rainforest is a valuable natural resource, which enables the country to earn much-needed income. The Malaysian government is under pressure from two sides – from industrialists who want to exploit the forest to increase the country's wealth and from conservationists who want to keep the forest.

▲ **K** Logging in Malaysia. About 4,000 km² of rainforest is felled every year in Malaysia. At this rate, the forest could disappear in 50 years.

Key

☐ Electronic components

☐ Crude petroleum

☐ Timber

▨ Rubber

☐ Palm oil

☐ Others

▲ **L** Malaysia's exports

---

3 Look at map J.

a) Estimate the percentage of land in Malaysia taken by each form of land use.

b) What differences do you notice between the Malaysian peninsula (Malaya) and the island of Borneo?

4 Look at pie chart L.

a) Estimate the percentage of Malaysia's export income from each product.

b) Which products came from the forest, or grow on land that was once forest?

Assignment

Work in groups of four. Each person will represent a different member of the Malaysian government (your teacher will give you more information to help you):

- Minister of Finance, who has to balance the money that the country spends and earns
- Minister of Environment, who has to protect the environment by using the forest sustainably
- Minister of Development, who has to improve the quality of life for everybody in Malaysia
- Minister of Culture, who has to look after the rights of different groups of people, like the Iban.

A foreign logging company wants to cut timber near Nanga Sumpa. Should it be allowed to chop down the forest?

a) Role-play the discussion at a meeting of ministers. Try to reach a decision.

b) Write a report to explain the decision that your group comes to.

5.7 Tourism – can we carry on like this?

In this case study you will think about the impact that tourism has on the environment and plan a more sustainable type of holiday.

Today, increased wealth and improvements in transport – particularly cheaper air flights – make it possible to go almost anywhere in the world. Travel programmes on TV encourage us to be more adventurous than ever before. It seems that tourism has no limits. Is it possible for us to carry on like this?

▲ **A** Machu Picchu, the lost city of the Incas in Peru, is one of the world's great tourist attractions ...

▲ **B** ... it's a shame about all the tourists!

Tourism is like other human activities – if it destroys the environment it is unsustainable. Sustainable tourism is tourism that does not harm the environment and benefits local people so that it can continue to be enjoyed by future generations.

Here are four questions that we need to ask before we book our holiday to decide whether it is sustainable.

How far is it and how will I travel?
The further you go the more fuel you will use. Planes use more fuel than other forms of transport and contribute most to global warming.

What impact will my holiday have on the local environment?
This could be anything from trampling on rare plants to dropping litter. Don't forget that things we take for granted here – such as water – may be scarce in some places.

Have local people been forced to move to make way for tourism?
In some countries, where tourist resorts or national parks have been created, local people have to make way for tourists and animals. Often, it becomes harder for them to survive.

Where will the money for my holiday go?
Most of the money you pay for a holiday goes to airlines or hotels, often owned by trans-national companies. If the money does not go to local people it is unlikely to benefit them or the local environment.

Activities

1 Look at photo A.
   a) Why do you think that so many tourists visit Machu Picchu?
   b) Would you want to go there? Give reasons.
   c) Now look at photo B. Does it make you more keen to go there, or less keen? Why?

2 Think of a place, or a country, you would most like to visit in your lifetime. Find out which country the place is in. For example, *Machu Picchu is in Peru.*
   a) Share your idea with the rest of your class. Make a list of all the places, or countries, your class want to visit.
   b) Mark the places on an outline map of the world, and label the countries.
   c) Which place or country do most people in your class want to visit? What do you think makes this place so appealing?

Homework

3 Think of a holiday that you have already been on.
   a) Try to answer the four questions for your holiday to find out how sustainable it was. Your parents may be able to help you. Do not worry if you can't answer all the questions.
   b) How sustainable do you think your holiday was? Explain your answer.

How could tourism become more sustainable?

Machu Picchu, the lost city of the Incas, was rediscovered about a hundred years ago. It immediately became a tourist attraction. Today it attracts over 500,000 visitors a year, and the number is growing by 6 per cent every year. Unfortunately, it is in danger of being destroyed by the impact of mass tourism.

2,000 people visit Machu Picchu every day. The site is being slowly eroded by the trampling of too many feet.

The number of people hiking the Inca Trail to Machu Picchu rose from 6,000 in 1984 to 82,000 in 2004.

Most tourists travel to Machu Picchu by train. There are plans to build a road up the valley and a cable car to the site.

The nearby town of Aguas Calientes has mushroomed in size, with more hotels and restaurants. Garbage is dumped in the valley and sewage pumped into the Urubamba River.

Helicopters fly in more tourists. They disturb the peace and quiet of the valley and could damage the site itself.

Steep slopes are eroded by heavy rains and landslides are common. The problem is worse where trees have been chopped down.

Hikers on the Inca Trail cut timber to provide fuel for cooking. There have been forest fires.

Tourism is not necessarily bad. It helps to create jobs and businesses for local people and it provides the Peruvian government with extra tax revenue. Machu Picchu and the Inca Trail generate about $10 million a year for Peru.

▲ **C** The impact of tourism on Machu Picchu and the Inca Trail

Around the world, different attempts are being made to make tourism more sustainable.

At the *Alhambra* in Spain they have changed the way that tickets are sold. Timed tickets restrict tourists to morning or afternoon visits and reduce crowds. Higher ticket prices have also reduced the numbers.

At *Stonehenge* in England they have reduced tourist access. The site is fenced off to prevent tourists from getting too close and causing damage. Tourists are guided to similar attractions that get fewer visitors.

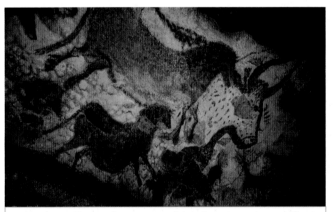

At *Lascaux* in France they have made replica cave paintings. The original paintings were being damaged, so the caves were closed and tourists now see a replica. People still feel as if they have seen the real thing.

Ecotourism is a form of tourism that brings people closer to nature and does no environmental damage. Of course, real ecotourists don't fly – they use more environmentally friendly forms of transport!

Activities

1 Study drawing C.
   In what ways is tourism at Machu Picchu unsustainable? Mention at least six things. You could write them on a spider diagram.

2 You are the Prime Minister of Peru. Would you encourage tourists to come to Machu Picchu or would you ban them? Give reasons for your answer.

Assignment

Study the ways in which tourism can become more sustainable on this page.

Either

Devise a management plan for Machu Picchu and the Inca Trail to make tourism more sustainable. Think about how many visitors you would allow, how they will get there, what they will be able to do and where they would stay.

Or

Plan a sustainable holiday for you and your family. It could be anywhere that you like, but remember, the further you go the less sustainable it is likely to be.

TEST YOURSELF

1 Which of these activities is more sustainable – riding a bicycle or driving a car? Explain your answer.

2 What is a national park?

3 Name the three national parks on this map of England and Wales.

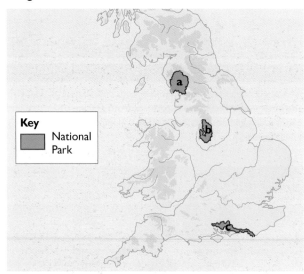

Key
National Park

4 a) What does conservation mean?
   b) Name two organisations in the UK that are involved in conservation.

5 Modern farming methods have contributed to the loss of birds in the UK countryside. How? Describe one example.

6 a) Complete this conflict grid for some of the activities in the countryside. Put an ✗, an ✓, or a 0 in each square to show conflict, harmony or no effect.

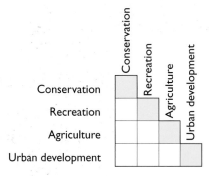

b) Choose one square with an ✗. Explain the conflict.

7 Complete this cross-section of tropical rainforest.

Scale

a) Label – emergent trees, canopy, undergrowth
b) Add a vertical scale to show the approximate height of the trees.

8 Describe three ways in which tropical rainforest is adapted to a hot, wet climate.

NOW, FOR A CHALLENGE!

9 For a named, natural environment that you have studied, explain:
   a) why the environment needs to be conserved?
   b) how the area can be managed to reduce the impact of human activities?

10 Tourism is not sustainable – agree or disagree? Answer this question by referring to a named case study.

These are the words you should try to learn for this unit:

TOP TEN WORDS

*sustainable   conflict   management
national park   conservation   habitat
tropical rainforest   ecosystem   adapt
tourism*

MORE KEY WORDS

*heritage coast
environmentally sensitive area
nature reserve   emergent trees   canopy
undergrowth   agriculture
recreation   urban development
ecotourism*

IMPRESS YOUR TEACHER!

*chalk downland   sustainable tourism
newly industrialised country (NIC)*

Unit 6

Tectonic Processes

Earthquakes and volcanoes

▲ An earthquake hit the Indian city of Ahmadabad in 2001

- What causes earthquakes, do you think?
- Why don't we get major earthquakes like this in Britain?
- From the photo evidence, would you say that India was prepared for the earthquake, or not?
- Can you ever be prepared for earthquakes? If so, how?

▲ A boy tries to pull his mother's body from the rubble

6.1   The world's worst disaster?

Earthquakes and volcanoes are natural hazards. They cause many of the world's worst disasters. On 26 December 2004 the world was shocked by one of the worst natural disasters ever. A powerful earthquake, measuring 9.0 on the Richter scale, near the island of Sumatra in Indonesia triggered a tsunami, or giant wave. About 300,000 people died in countries all around the Indian Ocean. (You can find out more about tsunamis on page 143.)

There have been bigger earthquakes in the past – one in Chile in 1960 measured 9.5 – and there have been higher death tolls – an estimated 650,000 died in an earthquake in China in 1976. However, no previous disaster has affected such a wide area, killing so many people in different countries at the same time.

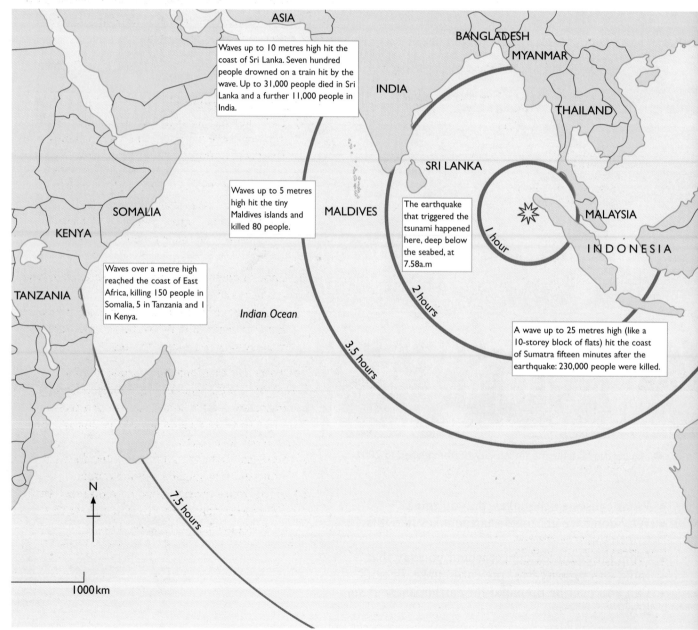

▲ **A** The impact of the Indian Ocean tsunami

▲ **B** A fishing boat stranded miles inland in Banda Aceh where it was carried by the tsunami

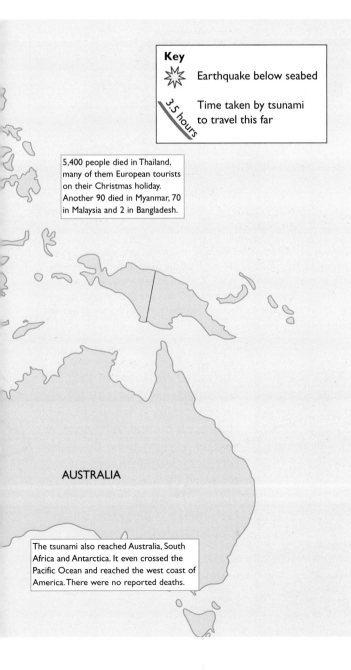

Key

✳ Earthquake below seabed

3.5 hours Time taken by tsunami to travel this far

5,400 people died in Thailand, many of them European tourists on their Christmas holiday. Another 90 died in Myanmar, 70 in Malaysia and 2 in Bangladesh.

AUSTRALIA

The tsunami also reached Australia, South Africa and Antarctica. It even crossed the Pacific Ocean and reached the west coast of America. There were no reported deaths.

Activities

1 Read this list of hazards.
   a) Sort them into two groups – *natural hazards* and *man-made hazards*. You could include some hazards in both lists.

   > air crash   avalanche   drought   earthquake
   > epidemic   explosion   fire   flood
   > forest fire   hurricane   landslide   tornado
   > tsunami   volcanic eruption   war

   b) Choose one hazard from each list. Explain why you put each one in that list.
   c) Look at your list of natural hazards. How could you sort them? Subdivide the list of natural hazards into two more groups.

2 You work for a national newspaper. It is 26 December 2004. Reports are coming in from countries around the Indian Ocean of a tsunami. You have to write a summary of the disaster for tomorrow's front page.
   a) Study all the information in A. Decide what information to include in your report.
   b) Write your report. It should be no more than 100 words. Make sure that you include the most important information.

6.2   Earthquakes

An earthquake is a sudden movement within the Earth. Earthquakes usually occur along faults, or cracks in the rock beneath the surface. In California, on the west coast of the USA, there are frequent earthquakes along the San Andreas Fault (photo A).

▶ **A** The San Andreas Fault is visible from the air, unlike most faults that are hidden below the Earth's surface

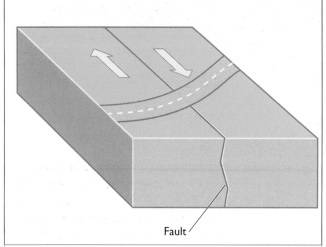

Fault

Forces deep in the Earth put pressure on rock near the surface. Sometimes, the rock on either side of a fault is being pushed in opposite directions. The huge slabs of rock get locked together and pressure builds up.

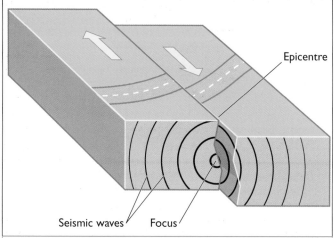

Epicentre

Seismic waves   Focus

Suddenly, at one point on the fault, the rocks give way and jolt past each other. This point is the focus of the earthquake. The energy, built up over months or years, is released and sends out vibrations, or seismic waves, through the rock. These are felt most strongly at the epicentre of the earthquake, on the surface directly above the focus.

▲ **B** How earthquakes happen

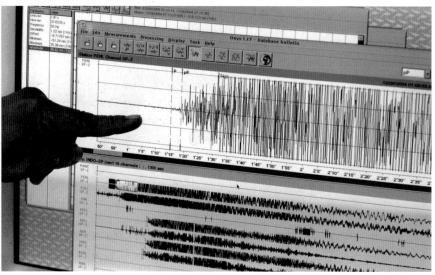

▲ **C** A seismograph

The closer the focus of the earthquake is to the surface, the more strongly it will be felt. Like ripples on a pond, the waves get weaker as they travel through the rock. Seismic waves are recorded on a seismograph. The amount of energy released by an earthquake is measured on the Richter scale (E).

Inside buildings floors move like jelly, ceilings fall down, furniture topples over, windows break and doors jam.

Bridges collapse and roads and railways split apart, bringing transport to a halt.

Gas pipes break and electricity cables are pulled down, causing fires.

Poorly designed buildings collapse and even well-designed buildings are damaged.

Water pipes break so water supplies are cut off.

Aftershocks can last for days after the main earthquake. It is dangerous to enter damaged buildings.

▲ **D** Earthquake damage from the Kobe earthquake in Japan in 1995

Measurement on Richter scale	Earthquake effects	How often they occur
Over 9	Devastation over an area thousands of kilometres across	One every 20 years
8.0–8.9	Major earthquake causing widespread damage over an area hundreds of kms across. At sea it may trigger a tsunami	One per year
7.0–7.9	Serious damage to buildings over an area hundreds of kms across. Bridges may collapse	18 per year
6.0–6.9	Damage to buildings over a wide area. Poorly designed buildings may collapse	120 per year
5.0–5.9	Some damage to buildings over an area tens of kms across	800 per year
4.0–4.9	Windows and doors rattle. Objects may fall over	6,000 per year
3.0–3.9	Slight vibration may be felt	50,000 per year
Less than 3	Too small to be felt but can be recorded on a seismograph	1,000 per day

▲ **E** The Richter scale

Activities

1 Study these pages. Find the correct word to match each of these meanings:
   • the point where an earthquake occurs
   • the vibrations from an earthquake
   • a sudden movement in the Earth
   • a crack in the rock below the Earth's surface
   • the point on the surface above an earthquake.

2 Look carefully at photo D and study the Richter scale in E.
   a) List the damage caused by the earthquake.
   b) Suggest what strength this earthquake measured on the Richter Scale. Give reasons.
   c) What problems might the rescue services, such as fire and ambulance, face in the aftermath of an earthquake like this?

Homework

3 Drop a pebble into a pond.
   a) Describe what happens on the surface of the water.
   b) What could this tell you about the seismic waves from an earthquake?

6.3 Volcanoes

Volcanoes are formed when magma, or molten rock, deep inside the Earth is forced up to the surface through a vent. When the volcano erupts, magma comes to the surface and is then called lava. It flows over the surface before it cools and solidifies. Ash and volcanic bombs may be blown out of the volcano's crater into the atmosphere.

Over time, layers of lava and ash build up to form a volcanic cone. Smaller vents may branch off from the main vent to form subsidiary cones. Mount Etna (photo A) was formed in this way. But volcanoes come in various shapes and sizes (photos C and D).

Mount Etna is an active volcano which, on average, erupts every few years. After many years lava from the volcano forms fertile soil for farming. About a million people live in the area around Mount Etna but few have been killed by the volcano.

Dormant volcanoes can be more dangerous. They may be quiet for hundreds of years, then erupt violently without warning.

Volcanoes that have not erupted for thousands of years are said to be extinct.

▲ **A** Mount Etna, a volcano on the Italian island of Sicily, seen from a satellite. The crater of the volcano is near the centre.

ITALY

Sicily ▲ Mt Etna

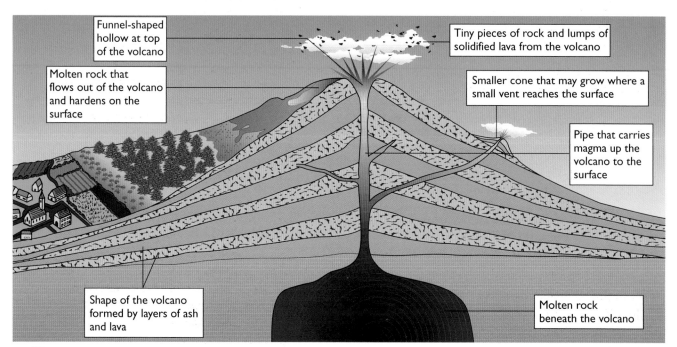

Funnel-shaped hollow at top of the volcano

Molten rock that flows out of the volcano and hardens on the surface

Shape of the volcano formed by layers of ash and lava

Tiny pieces of rock and lumps of solidified lava from the volcano

Smaller cone that may grow where a small vent reaches the surface

Pipe that carries magma up the volcano to the surface

Molten rock beneath the volcano

▲ **B** Cross-section of a volcano

▲ **C** A lava flow from Kilauea on Hawaii in the Pacific Ocean, an active volcano that erupts many times each year. The lava is runny and forms a gently sloping mountain, or shield volcano.

▲ **D** An ash cloud from the eruption of Mount St Helens in the USA, in 1980. The volcano had been dormant for hundreds of years. The lava is very thick, which caused the volcano to explode when it erupted. It forms a steep-sided cone volcano.

Activities

1 Look at drawing B.
 a) Match each description on the drawing to a blue word in the first two paragraphs on page 134.
 b) Draw your own labelled cross-section of a volcano. Replace each description with the correct word.

2 Look at satellite photo A.
 a) Use this colour key to work out what you can see in the photo:
   = lava flow/bare rock
  = natural vegetation
  = snow
  = settlement
  = farmland.
 b) Draw a sketch map of Mount Etna showing the main areas of each land use.
 c) Describe the pattern shown on your map. How do you explain it?

3 Read the following sentences from a scientist's diary. They describe what happened during an eruption of Mount Etna, but they have been muddled up.

a) Put the sentences in order.

> 1 Red-hot ash was thrown high into the air like a firework display.
> 2 Trees and farmland in the path of the lava were destroyed.
> 3 There was a huge explosion deep inside the volcano.
> 4 The volcano was rumbling and steaming as it does most of the time.
> 5 The lava thickened and slowed down and finally turned to solid rock.
> 6 The whole area was covered in a thin layer of ash as the cloud settled.
> 7 Suddenly the volcano became quiet and stopped steaming.
> 8 Lava poured out of the crater and began to flow down the side of the cone.

b) Compare Mount Etna with the volcanoes in photos C and D. Which volcano do you think is:
 i) most dangerous
 ii) most predictable?
 Give reasons for your answers.

135

6.4 Where do earthquakes and volcanoes happen?

In this case study you will test a hypothesis to explain where earthquakes and volcanoes happen. After your investigation you may want to rewrite your hypothesis.

1. I think that earthquakes and volcanoes only happen in hot places. The heat cracks the ground.

2. I think that they only happen on large continents. Britain is an island, and we don't get earthquakes or volcanoes.

3. They only happen in poor countries. People don't have the technology to prevent them.

4. I think you can get earthquakes and volcanoes anywhere – it's just a question of luck.

◀ A

Earthquake	Year	Strength on Richter scale	Deaths	Latitude	Longitude
North-west Turkey	1999	7.6	>17,000	41°N	30°E
Taiwan	1999	7.7	2,295	24°N	121°E
El Salvador	2001	7.7	850	13°N	89°W
Ahmadabad, India	2001	7.7	>20,000	23°N	72°E
Northern Algeria	2003	6.8	2,266	37°N	4°E
Bam, Iran	2003	6.6	26,000	29°N	58°E
Sumatra, Indonesia	2004	9.0	230,000	5°N	93°E
Kashmir, Pakistan	2005	7.6	>76,000	35°N	73°E

▲ **B** Some major earthquakes in recent years

Volcano	Year	Deaths	Latitude	Longitude
Mont Pelee, Martinique	1902	30,000	4°N	62°W
Novarupta, Alaska, USA	1912	0	58°N	154°W
Mount St Helens, USA	1980	57	47°N	122°W
Kilauea, Hawaii	since 1983	0	19°N	156°W
Nevada del Ruiz, Colombia	1984	23,000	5°N	76°W
Mount Pinatubo, Philippines	1991	800	15°N	121°E
Merapi, Indonesia	1994	43	7°S	110°E
Soufriere Hills, Montserrat	1995	20	17°N	63°W

▲ **C** Major volcanic eruptions in the past century

Activities

1 Look at the ideas around photo A.
   a) What do you think about these ideas? Are they right or wrong? Provide evidence to support your opinions.
   b) Write your own hypothesis (or idea) to suggest where earthquakes and volcanoes happen, and why. You will test this hypothesis through the rest of this case study to see if it fits the evidence.

2 Look at tables B and C.
   a) Find each of the places in the tables in your atlas. Use the latitude and longitude to find the exact locations.
   b) Locate and mark each one on a blank map of the world. It may help to number them on the tables and mark the number on the world map.
   c) Can you see any pattern on your map?

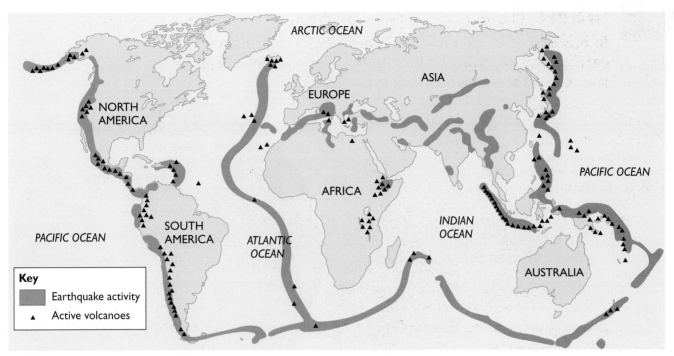

▲ **D** Areas of the world where there are earthquakes and volcanic eruptions

Key
- Earthquake activity
- ▲ Active volcanoes

▲ **E** The aftermath of an earthquake in Alaska

▲ **F** A volcanic island in Indonesia

3 Look at map D.
 a) Compare map D to your own map of earthquakes and volcanic eruptions. What do you notice?
 b) Describe the pattern on map D. Name the areas where earthquakes and volcanic eruptions happen.

4 a) Look back at the ideas around photo A. Use information on these two pages to disprove each of the ideas.
 b) Look again at your own hypothesis about where and why earthquakes and volcanoes happen. Does the information on these pages help to prove or disprove it?
 c) Now that you know more, do you need to rewrite your hypothesis? If so, do so now.

137

Why do earthquakes and volcanoes happen there?

You will have already noticed that most earthquakes and volcanic eruptions occur along narrow belts around the world. Look again at map D on page 137. Often they occur in the same places. This is more than just coincidence. To understand the pattern and the reasons for it, you need to know something about the Earth's structure.

Scientists believe that the Earth was formed from hot gases 4,600 million years ago, and that since then it has been slowly cooling down. Around the outside the crust, a layer of solid rock, has formed – rather like the skin on a bowl of custard as it cools. Compared to the rest of the Earth the crust is very thin. It has split into separate pieces known as plates. The line where two plates meet is a plate boundary.

The layer beneath the crust is called the mantle, where the rock is so hot that it is molten (like treacle). The plates float like rafts on top of the mantle. Heat from the solid core rises through the mantle creating convection currents that make the plates above move very slowly – usually no more than a few centimetres each year. Plates can move apart, collide or slide past each other.

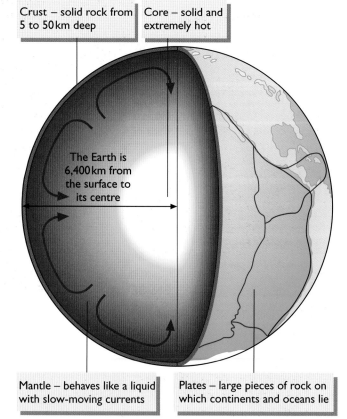

Crust – solid rock from 5 to 50km deep

Core – solid and extremely hot

The Earth is 6,400km from the surface to its centre

Mantle – behaves like a liquid with slow-moving currents

Plates – large pieces of rock on which continents and oceans lie

▲ **G** The Earth's structure

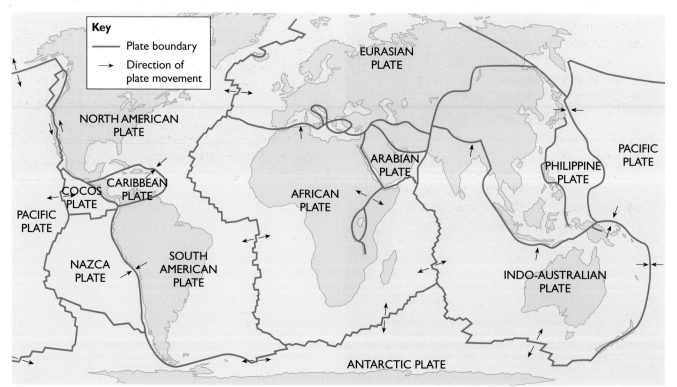

Key

— Plate boundary

→ Direction of plate movement

NORTH AMERICAN PLATE

EURASIAN PLATE

PACIFIC PLATE

ARABIAN PLATE

PHILIPPINE PLATE

PACIFIC PLATE

COCOS PLATE

CARIBBEAN PLATE

AFRICAN PLATE

PACIFIC PLATE

NAZCA PLATE

SOUTH AMERICAN PLATE

INDO-AUSTRALIAN PLATE

ANTARCTIC PLATE

▲ **H** The Earth's major plates

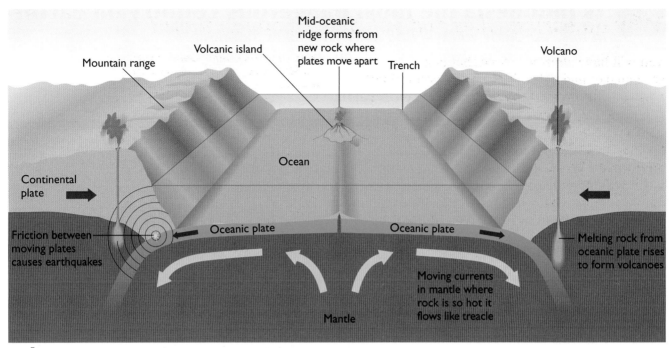

Mountain range

Volcanic island

Mid-oceanic ridge forms from new rock where plates move apart

Trench

Volcano

Continental plate

Ocean

Friction between moving plates causes earthquakes

Oceanic plate

Oceanic plate

Melting rock from oceanic plate rises to form volcanoes

Moving currents in mantle where rock is so hot it flows like treacle

Mantle

▲ I Cross-section of the Earth's crust

Activities

1 Look at drawing G. This shows the Earth's structure in three dimensions. Draw a cross-section of the Earth. Use the information on drawing G to make each layer the correct depth. Give your cross-section a scale.

2 Look at map H.
   a) Your teacher will give you jigsaw pieces of the Earth's plates. Make up the jigsaw to form a map of the world, and stick the pieces down.
   b) Compare your map with map D on page 137. Describe what you notice.

3 Look at drawing I.
   a) Explain why:
      i) earthquakes   ii) volcanoes
      are often found near plate boundaries.
   b) How does this help to explain your observations in activity 2b?

Assignment

Where do earthquakes and volcanoes happen?

Look back at your hypothesis. You tried to explain where and why earthquakes and volcanoes happen.

How close was your hypothesis to the reasons given on these two pages?

Write one or two paragraphs to evaluate your hypothesis.
• What were you right about?
• What were you wrong about?
Give evidence to show why your ideas were right or wrong.

Do you need to rewrite your hypothesis now? If so, how would you rewrite it?

6.5   Is Indonesia the most dangerous country on earth?

In this case study you will find out what makes Indonesia such a dangerous place to live. At the end you will carry out some internet research to help you to decide if it really is the most dangerous country on Earth.

Banda Aceh is the capital of the province of Aceh (say *Achai*) on the Indonesian island of Sumatra. About 320,000 people used to live there. At 8 a.m. on 26 December 2004 a major earthquake shook the town. Buildings were damaged and some collapsed. Yet, this was nothing compared to what followed. Fifteen minutes after the earthquake the tsunami struck (you have already read about it on pages 130–31). A 25 metre-high wave swept through the town destroying everything in its path. Half of Banda Aceh's population were killed along with thousands of other people along the coast of Sumatra.

▲ **A** Banda Aceh from the air before the tsunami

Activities

1 Look at photo A.
  Match these features with the letters on the photo:

  > a beach   fishing boats at a jetty   houses
  > a bridge   a school

2 Look at photo B. Compare it with photo A.
  Describe carefully what happened to each of the features you identified in A. For example, *The beach completely disappeared and the coastline moved back about 100 metres.*

Initially it was difficult to understand the scale of the disaster. But it was soon clear that Aceh was now a scene of total and utter devastation. Because the land in Aceh is low the water had entered right into the city. Ships were wrecked next to ruined buildings and cars were rammed against walls. Fishermen's houses were levelled and there were dead bodies everywhere.

▲ **B** Banda Aceh after the tsunami

3 You are one of the first journalists to arrive in Banda Aceh after the tsunami. Write a 200-word report for your newspaper about what happened. You can use any of the information on this spread

▲ **C** A survivor amidst the rubble of Banda Aceh

What can we learn from plate tectonics?

Indonesia is a country with more than 13,000 islands spread over an area the size of the United States (map D). It lies close to the boundary between two huge plates. The Indian Plate is moving slowly north to meet the Eurasian Plate. Indonesia has more active volcanoes than any other country.

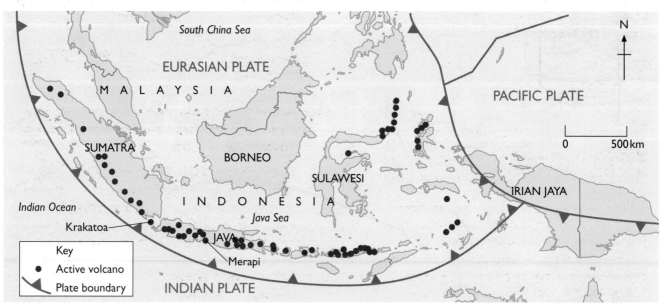

▲ **D** Active volcanoes and plate boundaries in Indonesia

Drawing E is a cross-section of the boundary between the Indian and Eurasian plates. Where the two plates meet, the heavier oceanic crust is forced down into the mantle. As the two giant slabs of rock try to grind past each other, they get stuck and pressure builds up. Suddenly, when the pressure gets too much, the plates jolt forward and earthquakes occur. Meanwhile, heat in the mantle melts the oceanic crust as it moves down. The molten rock is forced up, through cracks in the continental crust, forming volcanoes at the surface.

Activities

1 Look at map D.
   a) Describe the distribution of volcanoes in Indonesia. Name the islands where most volcanoes are found.
   b) Compare the distribution of volcanoes with the plate boundaries on the map. What do you notice?

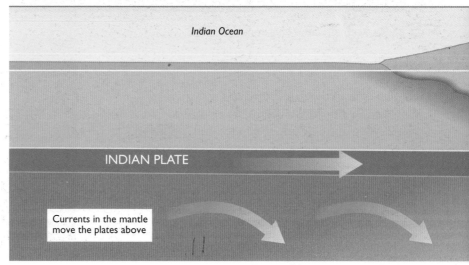

▲ **E** Cross-section of the boundary between the Indian and Eurasian plates

WHAT IS A TSUNAMI?

A tsunami is a huge wave caused by a sudden, violent movement on the sea floor. The Indian Ocean tsunami in December 2004 was caused by an earthquake off the coast of Sumatra, on the boundary of the Indian and Eurasian Plates. A section of the Eurasian Plate, which hadn't moved for years, was suddenly thrust upwards, releasing all of its energy. It displaced a vast amount of water in the ocean above to create the wave.

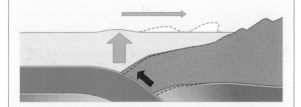

In the deep ocean a tsunami is a long, low wave that travels at up to 800 km per hour – the speed of a jet plane. Close to the shore, the sea gets shallower and the wave slows down. As the water piles up the wave grows higher, until it crashes into the land with immense, destructive power.

Activities

2 Look at cross-section E.
a) Draw a large copy of this cross-section. On it mark where, i) an earthquake ii) a volcano iii) a tsunami are likely to occur.

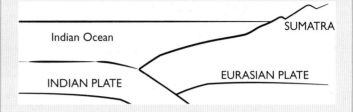

b) Explain why earthquakes, volcanoes and tsunamis occur close to the plate boundary. Write at least one sentence about each one.

3 Earthquakes and volcanic eruptions occur frequently in Indonesia. Carry out some internet research to find out what earthquakes and volcanic eruptions have happened recently in Indonesia. You can use these two websites for your research:
- http://earthquake.usgs.gov
- http://volcano.und.edu

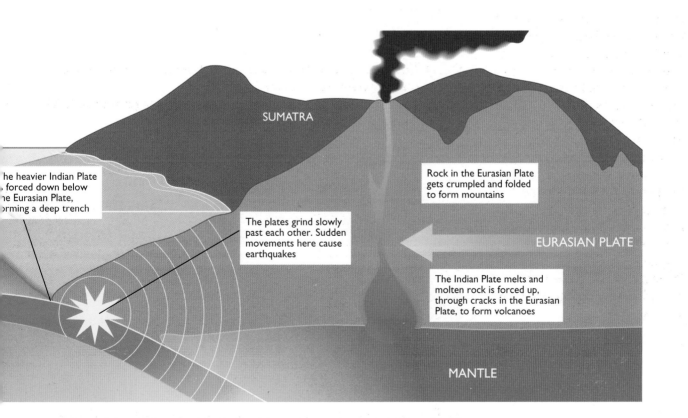

The heavier Indian Plate is forced down below the Eurasian Plate, forming a deep trench

The plates grind slowly past each other. Sudden movements here cause earthquakes

Rock in the Eurasian Plate gets crumpled and folded to form mountains

The Indian Plate melts and molten rock is forced up, through cracks in the Eurasian Plate, to form volcanoes

SUMATRA

EURASIAN PLATE

MANTLE

What has happened in the past?

Merapi is Indonesia's most active volcano (photo F). Over the past four hundred years it has erupted about sixty times. There was a major eruption in 1994. The dome of solidified lava at the summit exploded, sending a cloud of hot ash and gas – or pyroclastic flow – down the side of the volcano. Forty-three people were killed and 10,000 more were evacuated from villages. Merapi lies on Java, the most densely populated of all the islands in Indonesia.

▲ **F** Merapi – Indonesia's most active volcano

When Merapi erupts clouds of ash rise thousands of metres into the atmosphere. It covers the region in a blanket of ash that can ruin crops and lead to a shortage of food.

Nothing lives on the steep sides of the volcano. Pyroclastic flows travel up to 10 km from the summit at speeds of over 100 km/hour. They kill everything in their path.

Heavy rain mixed with ash can form mudflows up to 20 km from the summit. They pour down river valleys, burying everything in mud and drowning people.

However, it's not all bad. Lava and ash produce fertile soil, which is good for farming. That's one reason why so many people live close to the volcano.

Yogyakarta is a city with three million people just 30 km south of Merapi. When the volcano erupts dust and ash get everywhere so people need masks to breathe.

▲ **G** Merapi's impact on the island of Java

A BLAST FROM THE PAST

At two minutes past ten on the morning of Monday, 27 August 1883, Krakatoa, a volcanic island lying between Sumatra and Java, blew itself apart.

It was the most devastating eruption ever recorded. The sound was heard 5,000 km away, across the Indian Ocean. Dust from the explosion went high into the atmosphere and travelled around the world. It obscured the Sun and reduced temperatures worldwide by 1°C that year.

In Indonesia more than 36,000 people died. Most of them were killed by the tsunami that followed the eruption, as the island collapsed into the sea. The landslide created a wave 40 m high that destroyed towns and villages along the coast of Sumatra and Java.

Activities

1 Study the information in drawing G.
   a) Which dangers should each of these people be worried about? In each case, give a reason.
      • A scientist climbing the volcano to study its behaviour
      • A farmer living 15 km from the summit
      • A resident of Yogyakarta
      • An airline pilot flying over Java.
   b) If you were a farmer, would you continue to live near Merapi, or move away? Give your reasons.

2 Compare the eruption of Krakatoa in 1883 with the tsunami in 2004 (look back at pages 130–31 and 140–41).
   a) What similarities were there between the two events? Find at least two.
   b) What differences were there? Find at least two more.
   c) Could any lessons have been learnt from 1883 to prevent the disaster in 2004?

Assignment

You are going to carry out some internet research to find out if Indonesia really is the most dangerous country on Earth.

Go back to the websites you used for activity 3 on page 143.

a) Find out about major earthquakes and volcanic eruptions around the world in the past.
   How many of these were in Indonesia? How many people died? How does this compare to other countries in the world?

b) Find out more about recent earthquakes and volcanic eruptions around the world.
   How many of these are in Indonesia? How does this compare to the numbers in other countries in the world?
   Write a conclusion to your investigation.
   Is Indonesia more dangerous than other countries? Give evidence from your research to support your conclusion.

6.6 Ready for the Big One?

In this case study you will find out why San Francisco is threatened by earthquakes and suggest ways to make the city safer.

On Tuesday 17 October 1989 an earthquake measuring 7.1 on the Richter scale struck the city of San Francisco in California, USA. Sixty-seven people died. This was not the first earthquake that the city had experienced. In 1906 an earthquake measuring 8.1 virtually destroyed the city, killing 700 people.

▼ **A** Newspaper report following the San Francisco earthquake

STRONG QUAKE HITS SAN FRANCISCO

18 October 1989

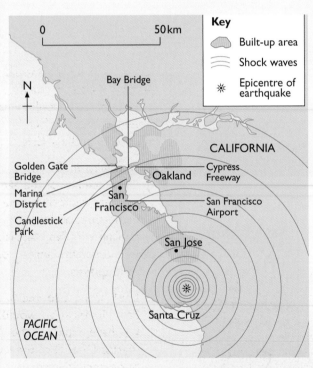

Key
- Built-up area
- Shock waves
- ☀ Epicentre of earthquake

Golden Gate Bridge
Marina District
Candlestick Park
Bay Bridge
Oakland
San Francisco
Cypress Freeway
San Francisco Airport
San Jose
Santa Cruz
CALIFORNIA
PACIFIC OCEAN

A major earthquake rocked the San Francisco region of California yesterday evening. The epicentre of the quake was about 100 km south-east of the city in the Santa Cruz mountains. At least sixty people are known to have died, with over 3,000 more injured. Thousands of people ran into the streets during the fifteen-second quake, which struck at the start of the evening rush hour at 5.04p.m.

Motorists were crushed to death when a section of a two-tier motorway – the Cypress Freeway in Oakland – collapsed. The road, which was meant to be earthquake-proof, shook like jelly when the quake hit. More people died at the Bay Bridge when part of the structure collapsed and cars fell into the water below.

At Candlestick Park, the San Francisco baseball stadium, 60,000 fans were packed in to watch an important game. There were screams as the whole stadium swayed for about fifteen seconds, opening up huge cracks. The game was called off and the stadium evacuated. Fortunately, no one was killed. San Francisco Airport was closed as a result of damage to the runway and buildings. At San Jose, closer to the epicentre, a shopping centre was badly damaged.

One of the worst affected areas of the city was the Marina District. Fires have been burning out of control in an area where many of the houses are built of timber. This area was destroyed by a previous earthquake in 1906.

Damaged homes in the Marina District of the city

San Francisco lies on the San Andreas Fault, a large crack in the Earth's crust that runs down the west coast of the USA (photo A on page 132). It is part of the boundary between two major plates. To the west the Pacific Plate is sliding northwards past the North American Plate to the east. Movement along the fault is only a few centimetres each year, but in some places the plates become 'locked' together. Tension builds up within the rock. An earthquake happens when the tension is released with a sudden movement along the fault (drawing B).

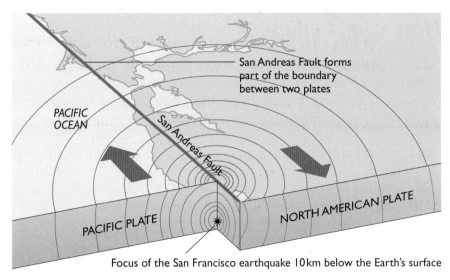

San Andreas Fault forms part of the boundary between two plates

PACIFIC OCEAN

San Andreas Fault

PACIFIC PLATE

NORTH AMERICAN PLATE

Focus of the San Francisco earthquake 10km below the Earth's surface

▲ **B** Plate movement along the San Andreas Fault

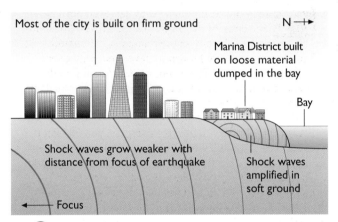

Most of the city is built on firm ground

N →

Marina District built on loose material dumped in the bay

Bay

Shock waves grow weaker with distance from focus of earthquake

Shock waves amplified in soft ground

← Focus

▲ **C** Cross-section of San Francisco

▲ **D** The Cypress Freeway collapsed in the earthquake

Activities

1 Read newspaper extract A. On a large copy of the map write labels to describe what happened at each place mentioned in the article.

2 Look at diagram B.
   a) Draw the line of the San Andreas Fault onto your map from activity 1.
   b) Explain why San Francisco is in constant danger from earthquakes.

3 a) Look again at source A. From its location, would you have expected the Marina District of the city to be badly damaged? Explain why.
   b) Look at drawing C. Now explain why the Marina District was so badly damaged.

How can prediction help?

Geologists use seismographs to measure the strength of the shock waves caused by earthquakes (see page 132). These are so sensitive that they can record even minor tremors that people do not feel. There are probably more seismographs along the San Andreas Fault than along any other fault in the world.

The number of earthquakes varies along the fault. Some stretches have frequent shocks, which show that the plates on either side of the fault are moving.

But there are also gaps along the fault, where there are few earthquakes. In these places the plates are locked together and tension is building up in the rocks, making a major earthquake more likely. This happened on the Loma Prieta Gap before the earthquake in 1989.

Geologists can now forecast the probability, or likelihood, of an earthquake at any point along the San Andreas Fault. Unfortunately, they cannot predict exactly when an earthquake will happen.

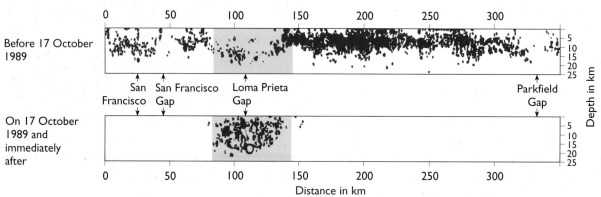

▲ **E** Earthquakes and tremors on the San Andreas Fault

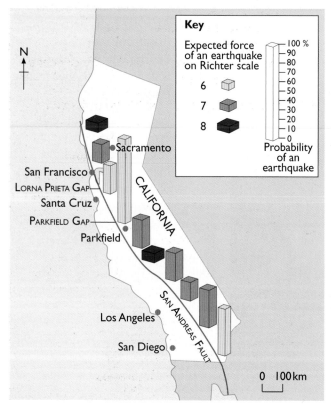

▲ **F** Earthquake predictions for California until 2025

Activities

1 Look at the graphs in box E.
   a) Describe the distribution of earthquakes and tremors shown in the first graph. Mention at what depth most earthquakes occur; the points along the fault where they mostly happen; where the gaps are.
   b) Where did the earthquake on 17 October 1989 happen? Why did it happen here?

2 Look at map F. Answer the questions:
   a) Where is the most likely place for the next earthquake?
   b) What (as a percentage) is the probability of an earthquake there?
   c) How strong is it likely to be (on the Richter scale)?
   d) Where is the most powerful earthquake likely to be?
   e) How strong will it be?
   f) What is the probability of this happening?
   g) How would you feel if you were living near the San Andreas Fault?

Assignment

Plan an earthquake-proof San Francisco

The California State Government wants to reduce the damage caused by future earthquakes in San Francisco. New buildings and roads must be earthquake-proof and old ones need to be strengthened. Vital buildings, such as schools and hospitals, should be in the safest areas, while the most dangerous areas should be reserved for parks and open space.

1 Your teacher will give you a large copy of map H and map I. Look at map H, which shows the seismic hazard, or danger from earthquakes, in each part of San Francisco. Seismic hazard is worked out from the type of rock in each part of the city and the distance from the San Andreas Fault.

2 Look at map I. It shows the main roads and public buildings in the city.

Trace your copy of this map to place over the seismic hazard map. Where seismic hazard is high, roads and buildings need to be strengthened. They should not be built at all where the hazard is greatest. Identify the sections of road and the major buildings that need to be strengthened. Highlight them on your map.

▲ **G** The Transamerica Pyramid in the city centre of San Francisco was built to withstand earthquakes. It is said to be able to sway up to 12 m without collapse.

3 Choose a suitable location for each of the following and mark them on your map.
   - a new hospital
   - a new waterside residential area
   - a new park
   - a route for a new railway linking the city centre to Candlestick Park.

4 Write a short report to explain your decisions.

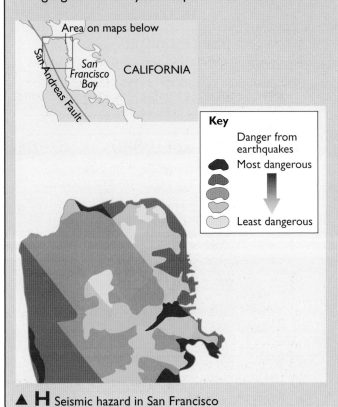

▲ **H** Seismic hazard in San Francisco

Key

Danger from earthquakes

Most dangerous

Least dangerous

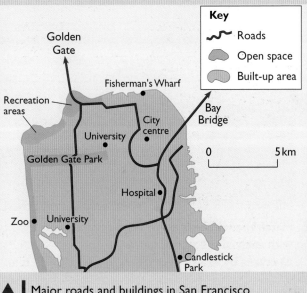

▲ **I** Major roads and buildings in San Francisco

Key

Roads

Open space

Built-up area

0 5km

Golden Gate

Fisherman's Wharf

Recreation areas

Bay Bridge

City centre

University

Golden Gate Park

Hospital

Zoo University

Candlestick Park

149

TEST YOURSELF

1 Name three natural hazards that are caused by tectonic processes (the movement of plates in the Earth's crust).

2 The Indian Ocean tsunami on 26 December 2004 was one of the world's worst disasters.
   a) Name five countries that were affected.
   b) What did the earthquake measure on the Richter scale?
   c) Roughly, how many people died?

3 What is an earthquake?

4 a) Complete this cross-section of an earthquake. Label – a fault, the focus, the epicentre, a seismic wave.
   b) Where will the earthquake be felt most strongly – in the village or the city? Explain why.

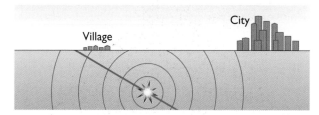

5 Choose a number (from 1 to 9) on the Richter scale to match the impact of each of these earthquakes:
   a) damage to buildings over a wide area
   b) devastation over an area thousands of kilometres across
   c) slight vibrations felt on the surface.

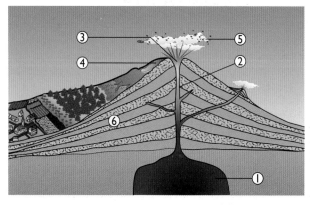

6 Match the numbers on this drawing of a volcano with each of the words below.
   a) crater b) lava c) vent d) magma e) ash f) cone

7 Write a paragraph to describe an eruption of the volcano in the drawing in question 6. Use all six words in your description.

8 Which is the odd one out in these groups of words? In each case, explain why.
   a) earthquake   hurricane   war   volcano
   b) fault   tremor   seismic wave   vibration
   c) ash   volcanic bomb   lava   magma
   d) active   crater   extinct   dormant

NOW, FOR A CHALLENGE!

9 Describe the global distribution of earthquakes and volcanoes. Mention which parts of each continent they are found in, e.g. along the west coast of North America.

10 Choose a named example of an earthquake or volcano you have studied.
   a) Draw a map to show its location, including plate boundaries.
   b) Write a paragraph to explain the causes of the earthquake or eruption.
   c) Write a paragraph to describe its impact, including its effect on people.

These are the words you should try to learn for this unit:

TOP TEN WORDS
*natural hazard   earthquake   focus
epicentre   volcano   magma   lava
crater   plate   plate boundary*

MORE KEY WORDS
*Richter scale   fault   tsunami
ash   volcanic bomb   vent   cone
subsidiary cone   active volcano
dormant volcano   extinct volcano
crust   mantle   core*

IMPRESS YOUR TEACHER!
*seismic wave   seismograph
shield volcano   pyroclastic flow
mudflow*

REVISE!

How to … Revise for your Common Entrance Geography Exam

You have come to the end of your Common Entrance Geography course. That was the enjoyable part. Now comes the bit that everyone dreads – the exam!

Don't panic. As long as you allow time to revise, it should not be any problem at all. We are going to show you six tried and tested techniques that you can use to revise. Some may suit you, some may not. Find out what techniques work best for you. Then use them to revise your geography course.

The secret of all successful revision is to make it **active** – not **passive**. This means that rather than simply trying to soak up information like a sponge, you do something that will really engage your brain. Find different ways to show the information you learnt. The more creative you can be, the easier it will be to remember.

ACTIVE | **PASSIVE**

Here are a few do's and don'ts when it comes to revision.

DO	DON'T
Make it visual – use drawings and diagrams	Re-read all your notes and expect to remember them
Summarise – pick out the key ideas	Copy out everything again
Map out your ideas – we call it mindmapping	Put your notes onto the computer (this is the same as copying)
Play with words – use memorable words, rhymes or phrases	Highlight or underline your notes with bright colours
Use stories – or create your own	
Test yourself	

1　A picture is worth a thousand words

Many of us have visual memories. We find it much easier to remember a drawing or a photo than we do to remember a lot of text. And, as luck would have it, a good geographical picture can contain just as much information as a page of writing.

　Do you remember how the sea erodes a headland? Below is the drawing you saw on page 7. It can help you to revise coastal erosion. Here's how.

1　Look carefully at the drawing. Try to memorise it.
2　Make your own copy of the drawing from memory.
3　Check that you put everything in the drawing. It doesn't have to be identical.
4　Annotate the drawing in your own words to explain what it shows (the drawing has all the clues you need to help you).

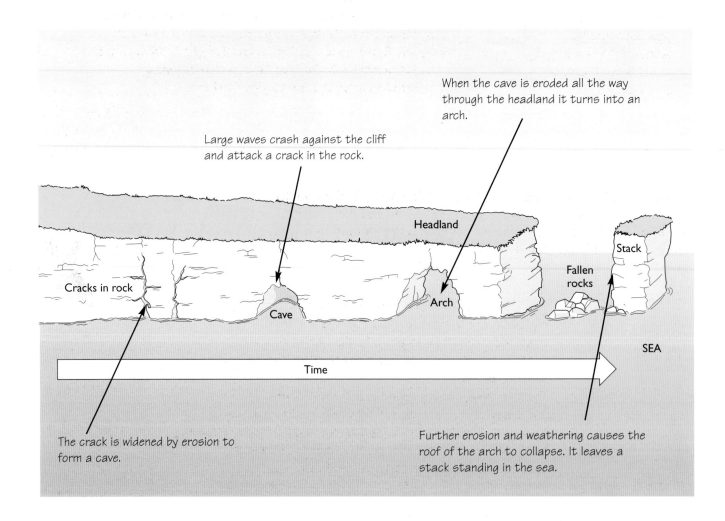

When the cave is eroded all the way through the headland it turns into an arch.

Large waves crash against the cliff and attack a crack in the rock.

Headland

Stack

Cracks in rock

Fallen rocks

Arch

Cave

SEA

Time

The crack is widened by erosion to form a cave.

Further erosion and weathering causes the roof of the arch to collapse. It leaves a stack standing in the sea.

2 Annotate your text

Just reading what you have written in your book does not guarantee that you will remember everything. A better way is to annotate your book in the margin at the side of the page. If you don't want to spoil your book by writing over it, you can annotate on post-it notes and stick them on your page. They will peel off later when you have finished revising.

Here is an example. In your work about settlements you wrote about Bristol's growth. Find the questions you answered in activity 1 on page 63.

A site is where the settlement was first built. A city is a very large settlement. The oldest part of a city is in the centre. Cities grow outwards If a settlement has a good site it is more likely to grow into a city.	a) The original site of Bristol was on the River Avon b) By 1850 the city had grown outwards from the centre. c) Since 1850 the city has grown further. It has continued to grow outwards and it has extended along the River Avon to reach the Bristol Channel. d) The River Avon was a good site for Bristol. It provided drinking water and, in the early days, it was also used as a means of transport. That helped the city to grow. Today Bristol lies close to the M4 and the M5. They provide a modern means of transport that helps the city to grow further.

Many pupils like to highlight or underline the notes in their books with a fluorescent pen. It is easy because you do not have to think too hard. But it is not really helping you to learn. Annotating your book is a much better way to revise.

	a) The original site of Bristol was on the River Avon. b) By 1850 the city had grown outwards from the centre. c) Since 1850 the city has grown further. It has continued to grow outwards and it has extended along the River Avon to reach the Bristol Channel. d) The River Avon was a good site for Bristol. It provided drinking water and, in the early days, it was also used as a means of transport. That helped the city to grow. Today Bristol lies close to the M4 and the M5. They provide a modern means of transport that helps the city to grow further.

3   Playing with words

Help! I've got to revise my geography.

In some subjects you just can't get away from learning words. Geography is one of those subjects. There is a lot of geographical vocabulary you need to know. To make life easier you can use *acronyms* (there's another word!). One acronym you probably know already tells you the colours of the rainbow in the correct order.

Richard Of York Gained Battles In Vain
(red, orange, yellow, green, blue, indigo, violet)

Staying with the topic of the weather, here is another acronym you could use to remember the processes that happen in the water cycle, in the order in which they happen (page 36).

Even Teenagers Can Panic Studying Geography!
(evaporation, transpiration, condensation, precipitation, surface flow, groundwater flow)

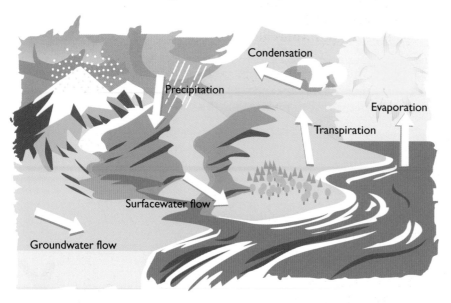

Another type of acronym uses the letters from just one word. For example, to remember the factors which affect a microclimate (page 34), think of the word *BASS* (as in *sea bass*).

B = buildings (buildings affect wind direction and absorb heat)

A = aspect (places that face the Sun are warmer than those in shadow)

S = surface (dark surfaces warm up faster and give off more heat)

S = shelter (sheltered places are less windy and get less rain)

The best acronyms are the ones you make up yourself. You are more likely to remember them. But don't worry if you can't think of one. If it takes more than five minutes to think of an acronym you're probably wasting valuable revision time.

4 Concept mapping

Concept mapping is a very appropriate way to revise geography! Like a normal map, a concept map is a quick way to help to find your way around a topic. Because concept maps are visual, and make use of colour, drawing and space, they are easier to remember than boring lists of facts.

Concept maps work particularly well for those topics that seem so big they are hard to get your head around. And they don't come bigger than globalisation (page 102)!

This is how you draw a concept map.

1 Write the main topic heading in the middle of your page, e.g. *Benefits of globalisation*
2 Think of important ideas linked with the topic. Write them around the main heading on the page. Draw lines, like branches, joined to the main heading. Use different colours.
3 Think of more ideas linked to the ones you have written. Write them down. Draw more lines, like twigs on each branch.
4 Keep the ideas as simple as possible – just one or two words at a time, if possible.

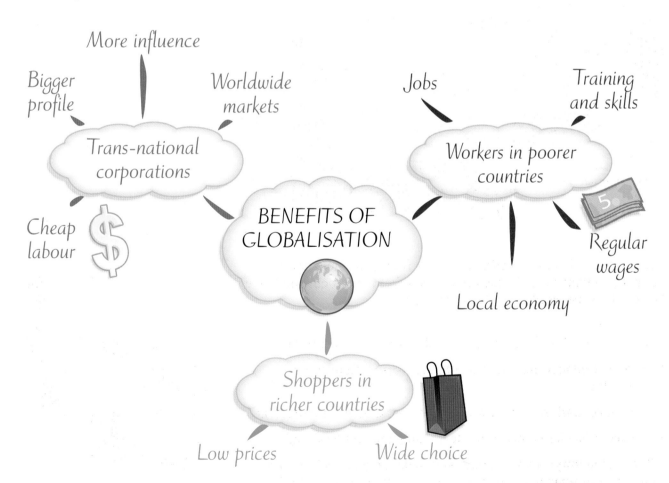

Now, you could do a similar concept map to show the *problems of globalisation*.

5 | Summary cards

Another way to summarise your notes is to write the key points down on small index cards (you can buy these in a stationery shop). This method has the advantage that you can carry the cards around in your pocket and read them at odd moments (but not in the exam, or you'll be disqualified!). It's not so easy to do that with a book.

If you're the sort of person that likes to be organised about revision, this is a good way to do it. Write a separate card for each topic that you have covered in geography.

You could divide the unit about Environmental Issues into summary cards like this. As a rough guide, write one summary card for each double-page spread in the unit. Include the key words from the unit.

Sustainable
– can be continued into the future because it is not wasteful.
People living in tropical rainforest have had a sustainable lifestyle for thousands of years. Our modern lifestyle is not sustainable.

Conflict
– conflict happens when different groups of people share the same environment

Management
– one way for lots of people to use the environment sustainably is to manage what happens.

National Park
– a large area of beautiful countryside that is protected by law.
National parks have three main aims:
● to conserve beauty, wildlife and heritage (conservation)
● to help visitors find out about the area and enjoy it (recreation)
● to meet the needs of local people for homes and jobs (local economy)

Conservation
– the way that we protect the environment. In the UK we have:
● national parks
● heritage coast
● environmentally sensitive areas
● nature reserves

Tropical rainforest
– the natural ecosystem in areas with a tropical climate
● covers 7% of world's land surface
● has a huge variety of plant and animal species
● each species is adapted to hot, wet climate

Tropical rainforest

● large evergreen leaves
● tall straight trunk
● lianas climbing up tree
● wide buttress roots

6   Everyone remembers a story

It's easier to remember stories than it is to remember lots of facts. That's because we identify with people in the stories and we get involved in what happens to them. You can learn a lot of geography from some stories. You can even use them to revise.

Some of the case studies in the book included true stories. For example, the story of the holidaymaker in Banda Aceh reminds us of facts about tsunamis (page 141).

> I was on a ferry between the island of Pulau Weh and Banda Aceh. I noticed that the ship bounced a little but I didn't pay any attention to it.
> I saw some people running on the shore but I didn't realise the scale of it all.
> In less than an hour we arrived in Banda Aceh and started to see that something out of the ordinary had happened. The jetties were submerged and some fishermen told us about a big wave.
> The scene was one of total and absolute devastation. The fishermen's houses were totally levelled. Everywhere there were corpses. Some people we met begged for food and water. They were all in shock.
> Banda Aceh is very low so the water went deep into the city. We walked for an hour witnessing big fishing boats that were thrown over buildings and more and more bodies that lined the streets. Cars appeared to be stuck to the walls, alongside the bodies of children and babies.

At sea, tsunamis produce only a low wave.

The wave travels at speeds of up to 800 km/hour. People have little time to escape.

In shallow water tsunamis slow down and water piles up.

Tsunamis hit the land with huge, destructive force.

You could also use a bit of imagination and make up your own stories. For example, you could use this photo of the Kobe earthquake (page 133) to make up a story to remind you of the impact that earthquakes have. It could start like this:
It happened early one winter morning when it was still dark. Mr Suzuki was still asleep in bed when the earthquake struck. The floor began to wobble like jelly...

Inside buildings floors move like jelly, ceilings fall down, furniture topples over, windows break and doors jam.

Bridges collapse and roads and railways split apart, bringing transport to a halt.

Gas pipes break and electricity cables are pulled down, causing fires.

Poorly designed buildings collapse and even well-designed buildings are damaged.

Water pipes break so water supplies are cut off.

Aftershocks can last for days after the main earthquake. It is dangerous to enter damaged buildings.

Answers to *Test yourself* questions

At the end of each unit in the book there is a *Test Yourself* section. You may have used them as you were doing your course or as part of your revision. When you finish each section you can check the answers here. No cheating!

Unit 1 Geomorphological processes

1 weathering – the breakdown of rocks
erosion – wearing away of the land
2 Water, wind and ice *or* three from – rivers, the sea, glaciers and wind
3 **a)** cave   **b)** arch   **c)** stack
4 **a)** Waves crash against the headland, eroding the rock to form a cave.
   b) When a cave is eroded all the way through the headland it turns into an arch.
   c) Further erosion and weathering cause the roof of the arch to collapse, leaving a stack.
5 Rivers erode, transport and deposit.
6 **a)** soft rock   hard rock   plunge pool
   b) Soft rock erodes more quickly
   Hard rock collapses into plunge pool
   The waterfall moves back
7 **a)** A glacier is a slow-moving river of ice
   b) Two from: a U-shaped valley, cirque, moraine
   c) Northern Britain. This was the part of Britain covered by ice during the Ice Age.
   d) Two from: Antarctica, Greenland, Himalayas, Andes or other mountain range.
8 **a)** *valley*   A valley is a landform. The other three are causes of landscape change.
   b) *source*   A source is the start of a river. The other three are jobs that a river does.
   c) *flood plain*   A flood plain is formed by deposition. The other three are formed by erosion.
   d) *U-shaped valley*   A U-shaped valley is a glacial landform. The other three are coastal landforms.

Unit 2 Weather and climate

1 Weather is the conditions in the atmosphere from day to day.
2 Each part of the UK has different weather. You should mention cloud cover/rainfall and temperature for your part of the UK.
3 **a)** You could record temperature, rainfall, air pressure, wind speed, wind direction or cloud cover.
   b) In the same order you would use a thermometer, rain gauge, barometer, anemometer, wind sock and mirror.
4 Buildings, ground surface, aspect and shelter.
5 evaporation, condensation, precipitation, surface flow (in that order)
6 **a)** Heat from the Sun warms the ground. Air above the ground rises and cools. Water vapour condenses to form clouds. It rains.
   b) Wind blows moist air from the sea over the land. Air is forced up over the hills. The air rises and cools. Water vapour condenses to form clouds. It rains.
7 **a)** The north of Britain is colder than the south because it is further from the Equator. The angle of the Sun is lower in the sky.
   b) The west of Britain is wetter than the east because the prevailing wind comes from the west. It brings moist air and rain.
8 **a)** *climate*   Climate is the average pattern of weather over many years. The other three are weather features.
   b) *cloud*   A cloud is a dense mass of water droplets. The other three are processes in the formation of cloud and rain.
   c) *weather*   Weather is day-to-day conditions in the atmosphere. The other three are factors that affect weather and climate.
   d) *rain shadow*   A rain shadow is an area sheltered from rain. The other three are types of rainfall.

Unit 3 Settlement

1 A settlement is a place where people live.
2 An urban area is built up. It has houses, tall buildings, factories, shopping centres, major roads and many people.
A rural area is countryside. It has open space, farms, fields, villages, trees, isolated buildings, narrow lanes and few people.
3 **a)** The best site is 3.
   b) It is close to the river for water supply and transport. It is on flat land. It is close to a bridge over the river.
4 **a)** From smallest to largest – hamlet, village, town, city.
   b) A hamlet has a phone. A village has a shop. A town has a supermarket. A city has a shopping centre and department stores. Any other example is OK.
5 True
False – small settlements are closer together than large ones
True
6 Convenience goods – bread, milk, newspaper or other examples
Comparison goods – clothes, furniture, electrical goods or other examples
7 central business district (CBD)   inner city   inner suburbs
8 **a)** CBD. This is where most clothes shops and department stores would be.
   b) Inner city. This is where the oldest housing is found.
   c) Outer suburbs. This is where the newest houses are found with more space for a garage.

Unit 4 Economic activity

1 A teacher, a cleaner and a headteacher are doing economic activities – paid work. A pupil is not.

2 a) Any six jobs, such as – manager, player, chief executive, accountant, programme seller, physiotherapist, etc.
   b) Any two other jobs, such as – police officer, coach driver, clothing factory worker, etc.

3 Primary – farmer
   Secondary – car assembly worker
   Tertiary – firefighter, plumber, footballer
   Quaternary – IT consultant

4 Raw materials, labour, power, market.

5 a) The best site is 3.
   b) It is closer to the sea for bringing materials in and out by boat. It is close to the motorway for transport. It is a large, flat site.

6 a) A trans-national corporation is a large company that operates in more than one country.
   b) Any three examples, such as McDonald's, Nike, Esso etc.

7 a) Two countries from south-east Asia, north Africa or central America, such as China, Tunisia or Mexico.
   b) Companies can employ labour more cheaply in these countries, in order to make greater profits.

8 A shopper in the UK might think, 'Globalisation is good. I can buy cheaper goods'
   A clothing factory worker in Asia might think, 'Globalisation is OK. I've got a job, but it doesn't pay me much'
   The head of a TNC might think, 'Globalisation is good. We make greater profits.'

Unit 5 Environmental issues

1 Riding a bicycle is more sustainable than driving a car because it does not use up fuel and does not pollute the air.

2 A national park is a large area of beautiful countryside that is protected by law.

3 a) Lake District   b) Peak District
   c) South Downs

4 a) Conservation is protection of the environment.
   b) Any two organisations, such as The National Trust, Royal Society for Protection of Birds (RSPB) etc.

5 Growing silage rather than hay means that farmers cut the grass more often. This destroys nesting sites for birds like the skylark. Or, you can give a different example.

6 a) Your conflict grid could look like this. You may have put Xs, ✓s or 0s in different squares. That's OK as long as you can explain why.

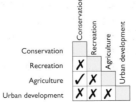

b) Conservation and urban development are in conflict because building destroys the natural environment. You can give any example.

7 a) emergent trees   canopy   undergrowth
   b) Vertical scale up to 50 metres

8 Any three from:
   Plants have evergreen leaves because it is hot all year round.
   Trees have tall, straight trunks to reach the light above the forest.
   Trees have wide buttress roots because the soil is shallow.
   Lianas (creepers) climb up trees to reach light.
   Few plants grow on the forest floor because it is dark beneath the canopy.

Unit 6 Tectonic processes

1 earthquakes   volcanoes   tsunamis

2 a) Any five from: Indonesia, Thailand, Sri Lanka, India, Myanmar, Malaysia, Maldives, Somalia
   b) 9 on the Richter scale
   c) About 300,000

3 An earthquake is a sudden, violent movement within the Earth's crust.

4 a) fault   focus   epicentre   seismic wave

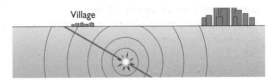

b) The earthquake will be felt most strongly in the village because it is closer to the epicentre.

5 a) 6 b) 9 c) 3

6 1 magma   2 vent   3 crater   4 lava
   5 ash   6 cone

7 Magma, or molten rock, deep inside the Earth is forced up to the surface through the vent in the volcano. When the volcano erupts the magma comes out of the crater as lava and pours down the sides of the volcano. Ash is blown out of the volcano into the atmosphere. Over time layers of lava and ash build up to form a volcanic cone.

8 a) war   War is a man-made hazard. The other three are natural hazards.
   b) fault   A fault is a crack in the Earth's crust where an earthquake can occur. The other three are caused by earthquakes.
   c) magma   Magma is molten rock inside a volcano. The other three come from the volcano.
   d) crater   A crater is the opening at the top of a volcano. The other three describe the state of the volcano.

Glossary

A

active volcano – a volcano that has recently erupted

adapt – to fit in, or change, to meet conditions in the environment

air pressure – the weight of air on the ground beneath it

alluvium – material deposited by a river on its flood plain

ash – fine particles of rock thrown from a volcano when it erupts

aspect – the direction in which a slope faces

atmosphere – the layer of air around the Earth

B

bay – an area of sea between two headlands

beach – material the sea deposits on the coast

biodiversity – the number and variety of all living things

biological weathering – the breakdown of rocks by plants and animals

bridging point – a place on a river where a bridge can be built

C

call centre – a large base for services, such as banking or insurance, that can be provided over the telephone

canopy – a top layer of trees that shade the forest floor from the sun

car assembly plant – a large factory where cars are put together

central business district (CBD) – the central part of a town or city where most shops and offices are found

channel – the space between two banks where a river flows

chemical weathering – the breakdown of rocks by chemical action

cliff – a very steep, rocky slope

climate – the pattern of weather over a long time

coast – the line between land and sea marked by high tide

cold front – a line where cold air pushes under warm air, causing heavy rain

comparison goods – things that we buy occasionally at the shops

competition – rival companies producing goods for the same market

condensation – the process of water vapour turning into water droplets

cone – a circular shape that rises to a point, typical of a volcano

conflict – disagreement, for example, between tourism and conservation

confluence – the point where two rivers meet

conservation – protection of the environment

contour line – a line joining places of the same height on a map

conurbation – a large urban area formed where settlements have merged

convection rainfall – rainfall formed when warm, moist air rises and cools

convenience goods – things that we buy often at the shops

core – the central part of the Earth, below the mantle

corrie – a circular hollow cut into a hillside by the action of ice

crater – a funnel-shaped hole at the top of a volcano

crust – the thin layer of rock that forms the outer part of the Earth

D

defensive town – a town built on a site that can be defended

deposition – the process of laying down material to form new land

depression – a moving area of low pressure, which usually brings rain

desert – an area with a very dry climate

desertification – the process by which an area turns into desert

development area – an area receiving government help to attract new industry

dispersed settlement – buildings spread out over a wide area

distribute – delivering goods over an area

dormant volcano – a volcano that has not erupted for many years

downstream – towards the mouth of a river

drought – a prolonged shortage of water

E

earthquake – a sudden, violent movement within the Earth's crust

ecological footprint – the amount of space needed to produce all the resources one person uses

economic activity – industry, or the way people earn their living

ecosystem – a community of plants and animals together with the environment in which they live

ecotourism – a form of tourism that helps to protect the environment

emergent trees – very tall trees growing above the forest canopy

Environment Agency – the organisation with responsibility for the environment in Britain

Environmentally Sensitive Area – an area where the beauty of the landscape depends on maintaining traditional farming methods

epicentre – the point on the surface above the origin of an earthquake

erosion – the process by which rocks are worn away

estuary – the mouth of a river where it widens to meet the sea

evacuate – move people from an area of danger

evaporation – the process of water turning to water vapour by warming

exploit – use, or develop, a resource for people's own benefit

extinct volcano – a volcano that has not erupted within historic times

F

fair trade – a system of trade that provides a better deal for farmers in poorer countries

fallow – a period when the soil is uncultivated and allowed to rest

fault – a crack or tear in the Earth's crust

fertile – rich in nutrients

fieldwork – an enquiry that takes place outside the classroom

flood plain – the flat area either side of a river that is regularly flooded

focus – the origin of an earthquake

frontal rain – rainfall cased by a depression, when warm air rises over cold air

function – the main activity or purpose, for example, of a town

G

geology – the study of rocks

glacier – a slow-moving river of ice

globalisation – the way jobs, people and ideas move around the world

gorge – a steep-sided valley

groyne – a barrier built out into the sea to slow movement of material along a beach

H

habitat – a place where animals or plants live

hamlet – a very small settlement without services

headland – land that juts out into the sea

Heritage Coast – a stretch of beautiful coast that is protected

I

ice sheet – a huge mass of ice that completely covers the land

impermeable – does not allow water to pass through

industrial town – a town that has grown around a manufacturing industry

industry – an economic activity, or type of work

inner city – the area of a city around the city centre

inner suburb – an older suburb, closer to the city centre

intermediate area – an area, like a development area, that receives some government help to attract industry

irrigation – the supply of water to land by means of canals, pipes and sprinklers

isobar – a line on a weather map joining places with equal air pressure

L

labour – people who work

landform – a natural feature of the landscape

lava – molten rock from a volcano

less economically developed countries (LEDCs) – poorer countries with low GNP (Gross National Product) per capita

levee – a raised river embankment that helps to prevent flooding

Linear settlement – buildings in a line, usually in a valley or along a road

longshore drift – the movement of material along the coast

M

magma – molten rock found beneath a volcano

mantle – the middle layer of the Earth between the crust and the core

manufacturing – making products, usually in a factory

market – a place where goods are sold or, at a wider scale, the people who buy the goods

market town – a town that originally grew around a market, where people bought and sold goods

meander – a bend in a river

Mediterranean climate – a climate with hot, dry summers and mild, wet winters

Meteorological Office – the organisation that forecasts weather in Britain

meteorologist – a person who studies the weather

microclimate – the climate found in a very small area

mining – extracting primary resources from the ground

moraine – rocks and stones deposited by a glacier when it melts

more economically developed countries (MEDCs) – richer countries with high GNP (Gross National Product) per capita

mudflow – the movement of soil or ash, carried by heavy rain or melting snow

N

national park – a large area of beautiful countryside that is protected by law

natural hazard – a natural event that creates danger for people, such as an earthquake or flood

natural resource – something that can be grown, found in the sea, or dug from the ground

nature reserve – a natural area where wildlife is protected from human activities

Newly Industrialised Country (NIC) – a country that has recently become industrialised

nucleated settlement – buildings grouped together

O

outer suburb – a modern suburb, closer to the edge of a city

P

physical weathering – the breakdown of rock by changes of temperature

plate – a large segment of the Earth's crust

plate boundary – the line where two plates meet

plate tectonics – the movement of plates as they float on the molten rock in the mantle beneath

port – a place where ships load and unload, and the settlement around it

power – energy

precipitation – rain, drizzle, snow, sleet or hail

primary activities – the way natural resources are obtained from the land or the sea process – the way something happens

pyroclastic flow – a volcanic cloud of hot ash and gases moving at high speed down slopes

Q

quaternary activity – a high-tech service that provides information or expertise

R

rain shadow – the side of a hill, sheltered from the wind, where less rain falls

raw material – a natural resource used to make a product

recreation – leisure activity

recyling – re-using resources again and again

relief – the shape of the land

relief rainfall – rain caused by air being forced up, over hills and mountains

reservoir – an artificial lake used to store water

resort – a town where people go for holidays

retail – selling products to the public

Richter scale – the scale used to measure the strength of earthquakes

run-off – rainfall carried off an area by streams and rivers

rural – of or in the countryside

S

sea wall – a barrier built behind a beach to protect the coast from the sea

secondary activity – manufacturing (making products from natural resources)

sediment – fragments of rock that are deposited by water, ice or wind

sedimentary rock – rock formed from material laid down millions of years ago at the bottom of seas and lakes

seismic wave – a tremor, or vibration, caused by an earthquake

seismometer – an instrument to measure Earth movements

service – tertiary industry (activities that meet people's needs but produce no end product)

settlement – a place where people live

settlement hierarchy – the order of importance of settlement

shield volcano – a gently sloping volcano that has been formed from runny, fast-flowing lava

site – a place to build on

source – the beginning of a river

stack – a pillar of rock that stands in the sea

subsidiary cone – a smaller cone that may grow on the side of a larger volcano

suburb – an area near the edge of a town or city that is mainly low-density housing

sustainable – something that can be continued because it is not wasteful

sustainable development – development that can meet present and future needs

T

temperate – not extreme, neither very hot nor very cold

terminal moraine – rocks and stones deposited at the end of a glacier when it melts

terraced houses – houses that are joined together

tertiary activity – services (activities that meet people's needs but produce no end-product)

tourism – a service industry providing holidays for people

trans-national corporation (TNC) – a very large company with branches in more than one country

transport – moving (goods) from one place to another

transportation – the movement of material by water, ice or wind

tremor – a small earthquake, or vibration, in the Earth's crust

tropical rainforest – tall, dense forest found in hot, wet areas

tsunami – a huge wave often caused by an earthquake on the ocean floor

U

undergrowth – small trees and bushes growing on a forest floor

unemployment – lack of employment or work

unsustainable – something that cannot continue because it is wasteful

upstream – towards the source of a river

urban – of or in a built-up area

urban regeneration – redevelopment of a city to bring it back to life

U-shaped valley – a deep, steep-sided valley that was eroded by a glacier

V

vent – a pipe that carries magma to the surface of a volcano

volcanic bomb – a lump of solidified lava thrown from a volcano when it erupts

volcano – a cone-shaped mountain formed from lava and/or ash

V-shaped valley – valley eroded by a river with a V-shaped cross-section

W

warm front – a line where warm air rises over cold air, giving prolonged rain

water cycle – the movement of water between the sea, land and air

water store – a place where water is stored in the water cycle

water vapour – water in the form of an invisible gas

waterfall – a point on a river where water falls vertically

wave – circular motion of water caused by wind

weather – the condition of the atmosphere from day to day

weather station – a collection of instruments used to record the weather

weathering – the breakdown of rocks

Index